RAMBLES

OF

A NATURALIST.

WITH A

MEMOIR OF THE AUTHOR,

DR. JOHN D. GODMAN.

PHILADELPHIA:
PUBLISHED BY THE
ASSOCIATION OF FRIENDS FOR THE DIFFUSION OF RELIGIOUS
AND USEFUL KNOWLEDGE,
109 NORTH TENTH STREET.
1859.

THE account of the life and character of DR. JOHN D. GODMAN has been prepared from the several brief memoirs and eulogies published shortly after his decease, and from the tract issued by "The Tract Association of Friends," entitled "A Sketch of the Life and Character of Dr. John D. Godman."

"The Rambles of a Naturalist" have been republished from "The Friend," a weekly paper, for the columns of which the essays were originally contributed.

MEMOIR

OF

DR. JOHN D. GODMAN.

DR. JOHN D. GODMAN, the author of the pleasing descriptions which, under their simple title, "Rambles of a Naturalist," contain so much of the beautiful and true, was born at Annapolis, in Maryland, in the year 1798. At a very early age he was deprived, by their death, of both his parents. He was then placed under the care of an aunt, whose intellectual attainments and elevated piety, united to much sweetness of disposition, eminently qualified her for the direction of the youthful mind. His fondness for books and aptitude for learning were remarkable; while his frank, sensitive, and sweet temper gained the affection of all around him. It is said that he had such a reverence for truth, even from infancy, that he was never known to equivocate. When he attained the age of six years, his excellent aunt died. The patrimony which should have provided for his wants, was lost through the mismanagement of those to whom the care of it had been entrusted; and thus, without resources, and without suitable protection, he was left exposed to adversity and temptation. It appears, however, that the moral and religious impressions which had already been made upon his mind, though obscured for a time, were never obliterated. In his last illness he bore this testimony to the affectionate religious care of his pious aunt. "If," said he, "I have ever been led to do any good, it has been through the influence of her example, instruction, and prayers."

Little is known of the next ten years of his life. He appears to have had some opportunities for attending school; but to his own native energy and uncommon intellectual endowments, self cultured under many obstacles and discouragements, is his future superiority of mental attainment to be chiefly attributed. An interesting incident of his character, after he had attained his fifteenth year, has been furnished by a physician who was, in 1810, a senior student in the office of Dr. Thomas E. Bond, of Baltimore. "The office," says he, "was fitted up with taste, and boys, attracted by its appearance, would frequently drop in to gaze on the labelled jars and drawers. Among them I discovered one evening an interesting lad, who was amusing himself with the manner in which his comrades pronounced the 'hard words' with which the furniture was labelled. He appeared to be quite an adept in the Latin language. A strong curiosity soon prompted me to inquire, 'What is your name, my little boy?' He was small of his age. 'My name is John D. Godman.' 'Did you study the Latin language with Mr. Creery?' 'No, he does not teach any but an English school.' 'Do you intend to prosecute your studies alone?' 'I do; and I will, if I live, make myself a Latin, Greek, and French scholar.'"

In 1812 he was bound an apprentice to a printer of a newspaper, in Baltimore, but soon became much dissatisfied with the occupation, which, he said, in a letter to a friend, "cramped his genius over a font of types, where there are words without ideas." He had been placed in this situation against his own wish, being anxious to enter a more intellectual pursuit, and had selected that of medicine; but his guardian was opposed to it.

His early views of the Christian religion are thus expressed in a letter to a friend, in the early part of 1814: "I have not ever had a fixed determination to read the works of that modern serpent (Thomas Paine), nor had I determined not to do it; and it seems to me surprising that a fellow-student of yours should recommend the perusal of such writings.

"There is a great comfort in the belief of that glorious doctrine of salvation that teaches us to look to the Great Salvator for happiness in a future life; and it has always been my earnest desire, and I must endeavour to die the death of the righteous, that my last end and future state may be like His. It would be a poor hope indeed, it would be a sandy foundation for a dying soul, to have no hope but such as might be derived from the works of Bolingbroke and Paine; and how rich the consolation and satisfaction afforded by the glorious tidings of the blessed Scriptures! It is my opinion there has never one of these modern deists died as their writings would lead us to believe; nor are but few of their writings read at the present day."

About this time he appears to have left the printing-office, and became a sailor on board the flotilla stationed in Chesapeake bay, under Com. Barney. It was while in this situation that an incident occurred to which he has himself attributed much of the buoyancy and energy of his character. A raw sailor, who had been sent aloft by the captain, and was busy in performing some duty which required him to stoop, was observed to falter and grow dizzy. "*Look aloft,*" cried the captain; and the fainting landsman, as he instinctively obeyed the order, recovered his strength and steadiness. The young philosopher read a moral in this trifling incident which he never forgot, and which frequently animated and aroused him in the most adverse circumstances. It is not treating the subject with undue levity to add, that in the last and closing scene of his life, when the earth was receding from his view, and his failing strength admonished him of his peril, the watchword was still ringing in his ear. At that awful period he "looked aloft" to "worlds beyond the skies," and therein derived strength and hope, which supported him in his passage through the narrow valley

At the close of the war, young Godman received an invitation from Dr. L., the physician already mentioned, to come to his house in Elizabethtown, Pa., where he would have the opportunity of studying medicine. This offer was accepted with joy; and he resolved, by the most indefatigable study and diligence, to deserve the kindness of his friend. "In six weeks," says the doctor, "he had acquired more knowledge in the different departments of medical science, than most students do in a year. During this short period he not only read Chaptal, Fourcroy, Chesselden, Murray, Brown, Cullen, Rush, Sydenham, Sharp, and Cooper, but wrote annotations on each, including critical remarks on the incongruities in their reasonings. He remained with me five months, and at the end of that time you would have imagined from his conversation that he was an Edinburgh graduate." When he sat down to study, he was so completely absorbed by his subject, that scarcely any event would withdraw his attention.

Returning to Baltimore, he commenced the attendance of the medical lectures in that city, and pursued his studies under the direction of an eminent medical preceptor. In this situation he, through many affecting difficulties, finished his education as a physician. At one time his feelings are thus described in a letter: "I have been cast among strangers. I have been deprived of property by fraud that was mine by right. I have eaten the bread of misery. I have drunk of the cup of sorrow. I have passed the flower of my days in a state little better than slavery, and have arrived at what? Manhood, poverty, and desolation. Heavenly Parent, teach me patience and resignation to Thy will!"

Professor Sewall, in his eulogy on Dr. Godman, remarks, in relation to this period of his life: "He pursued his studies with such diligence and zeal as to furnish, even at that early period, strong intimations of his future eminence. So indefatigable was he in the acquisition of knowledge, that he left no opportunity of advancement unimproved; and, notwithstanding the deficiencies of his preparatory education, he pressed forward with an energy and perseverance that enabled him not only to rival, but to surpass all his fellows."

While attending his last course of lectures in the University of Maryland, Professor Davidge, who was his preceptor, was disabled by the fracture of a limb from completing the course. He selected his gifted pupil to supply his place. "This situation he filled for several weeks with so much propriety; he lectured with such enthusiasm and eloquence; his illustrations were so clear and happy, as to gain universal applause. At the time he was examined for his degree, the superiority of his mind, as well as the extent and accuracy of his knowledge, were so apparent, that he was marked by the professors of the university as one who was destined at some future period to confer high honour upon the profession."

Dr. Godman graduated in the Second month, 1818, and soon after settled in Maryland, as a practitioner, in a county bordering on the Chesapeake, the spot described with so much truthful beauty in some of the numbers of his "Rambles of a Naturalist." Here he devoted all the intervals of leisure from a laborious practice to the study of natural history, in which, from his ardent love of the subject, and his minute, persevering investigation of it, he became so distinguished.

His intellectual powers had fitted him for a wider sphere than that of a village doctor. His nature urged him to enter on a field more worthy of his gifts. He returned to Baltimore, with the hope of being engaged in the university as a professor, but found that arrangements different from what he anticipated had been made. Here he married, and not long after received an appointment to fill the chair of surgery in the medical college of Ohio, located at Cincinnati. He was recommended by one of the professors of the school in which he had been educated, in this emphatic language: "In my opinion, Dr. Godman would do honour to any school in America."

The Ohio school not succeeding, Dr. Godman resided in Cincinnati for one year only; but in that short period inscribed himself deeply on the public mind. The memory of his works remains. In the midst of his varied scientific labours, he found time to cultivate his social relations, and every day added a new friend to the catalogue of those who loved him for his simplicity and frankness, not less than they admired him for his genius, vivacity, and diligence.

He returned to Philadelphia, and soon after began to lecture on anatomy and physiology, his first and greatest objects. His residence in this city continued for several years, during which time he wrote many valuable papers on scientific subjects, and published his celebrated work, "The Natural History of American Quadrupeds," which has attained deserved popularity.

The fame of Dr. Godman as a teacher of anatomy was now widely spread, and he was solicited to accept the professorship of that branch in the Rutgers Medical College at New York. His practice soon became extensive, and the affairs of the college prosperous, when, in the midst of his second course of lectures, a severe cold settled on his lungs, accompanied by a copious hemorrhage, and compelled him to abandon his pursuits, and flee for his life to a milder region. He sailed for the West Indies, and passed the remainder of the winter and spring in the island of Santa Cruz. Returning after this to Philadelphia, he took a house in Germantown, and by the labours of his pen, continued to support his family. His consumptive disease continued, though for a time so far mitigated, that his friends flattered themselves his life was yet to be spared to science and his country. At this time he says of himself: "At present, that I am comparatively well, my literary occupations form my chief pleasure; and all the regret I experience is, that my strength is so inadequate to my wishes. Should my health remain as it is now, I shall do very well; and I cannot but hope, since we have recently passed through a severe spell of cold weather without my receiving any injury. All my prospects as a public teacher of anatomy are utterly destroyed, as I can never hope, nor would I venture if I could, again to resume my labours. My success promised to be very great, but it has pleased God I should move in a different direction."

His disease advanced with steady pace, and, though there were many fluctuations, his strength continued to decline. The gradual progress of his disorder allowed him many intervals of comparative ease. In these he returned to his literary labours with his usual ardour, and wrote and translated for the press until within a few weeks of his death. Perfectly aware of the fatal character of his disorder, he watched its progress step by step with the coolness of an anatomist, while he submitted to it with the resignation of a Christian. The "Rambles of a Naturalist" were among the last productions of his pen, and were written in the intervals of acute pain and extreme debility. These essays are not inferior in poetical beauty, and vivid and accurate description, to the celebrated letters of Gilbert White on the natural history of Selbourne. He came to the study of natural history as an investigator of facts, and not as a pupil of the schools; his great aim being to learn the instincts, the structure, and the habits of all animated beings. This science was a favourite pursuit, and he devoted himself to it with indefatigable zeal. He has been heard to say that, in investigating the habits of the shrew mole, he walked many hundred miles. His powers of observation were quick, patient, keen, and discriminating: it was these qualities that made him so admirable a naturalist.

His fame, however, rested chiefly, during his life, upon his success as a teacher of anatomy, and in this capacity he raised himself at once to the top of his profession. He was so intent on making his students understand him, and he was so fully master of the subject himself, that his clear and animated flow of eloquence never failed to rivet their attention; and he became, wherever he taught, the idol of his pupils. His lectures on anatomy were real analytical experiments. The subject was placed before the class; tissue and muscle and blood, vessel and bone, were laid bare in their turn, their use and position exemplified to the eye, and enforced by the most lively and precise description; while the student was at the same time receiving the most valuable lessons in practical dissection.

Dr. Godman had a remarkable capacity for concentrating all his powers upon any given object of pursuit. What he had once read or observed he rarely, if ever, forgot. Hence it was that, although his early education was much neglected, he became an excellent linguist, and made himself master of Latin, French, and German, besides acquiring a knowledge of Greek, Italian, and Spanish. He had read the best works in these languages, and wrote with facility the Latin and French. His character and acquirements are justly portrayed by a distinguished journalist, in the extracts which follow. "The tributes," said he, "which have been paid in the newspapers to the late Dr. Godman, were especially due to the memory of a man so variously gifted by nature, and so nobly distinguished by industry and zeal in the acquisition and advancement of science. He did not enjoy early opportunities of self-improvement, but he cultivated his talents, as he approached manhood, with a degree of ardour and success which supplied all deficiencies; and he finally became one of the most accomplished general scholars and linguists, acute and erudite naturalists, ready, pleasing, and instructive lecturers and writers, of his country and era. The principal subject of his study was anatomy in its main branches, in which he excelled in every respect. His attention was much directed also to physiology, pathology, and natural history, with an aptitude and efficiency abundantly proved by the merits of his published works, which we need not enumerate.

We do not now recollect to have known any individual who inspired us with more respect for his intellect and heart, than Dr. Godman; to whom knowledge and discovery appeared more abstractly precious; whose eye shed more of the lustre of generous and enlightened enthusiasm; whose heart remained more vivid and sympathetic amidst professional labour and responsibility, always extremely severe and urgent. Considering the decline of his health for a long period, and the pressure of adverse circumstances, which he too frequently experienced, he performed prodigies as a student, an author, and a teacher; he prosecuted extensive and diversified researches; composed superior disquisitions and reviews, and large and valuable volumes; and in the great number of topics which he handled simultaneously, or in immediate succession, he touched none without doing himself credit, and producing some new development of light, or happy forms of expression. He lingered for years under consumption of the lungs; understood fully the incurableness of his melancholy state; spoke and acted with an unfeigned and beautiful resignation; toiled at his desk to the last day of his thirty-two years, still glowing with the love of science and the domestic affections."

Upon all this bright attainment and brighter promise for the future the grave has closed. Divine Providence saw fit to arrest him in the midst of his unfinished labours. We have now to view him in another and far more important relation—that which man, as an immortal being, bears to his Almighty Creator.

Dr. Godman's generous and enthusiastic devotion to science and learning commands our admiration; and perhaps no more ennobling pursuits can occupy the mind of him who looks not beyond the present state of existence; but when these are brought into contrast with the solemn and momentous concerns of eternity, they sink into utter insignificance. How then was the subject of this memoir influenced by *religious* considerations?

Unhappily, the philosophical and religious opinions of Dr. Godman were formed originally in the school of the French naturalists of the last century. Many of the most distinguished of these men were avowed atheists, and a still greater number rejected absolutely the Christian revelation. Such is fallen human nature! Surrounded by the most magnificent displays of Almighty Wisdom — placed on a scene where all things speak of God, and invite us to worship and obey Him — a purblind philosophy may devote herself to the study of His works, yet pass by the testimony they furnish of His existence and attributes, and see nothing in all this wonderful creation more noble than the mere relations of colour and form. It was so with Dr. Godman; for, while assisted by such lights as these, and guided alone in his investigations by perverted reason, he became, as he tells us, *an established infidel,* rejecting revelation, and casting all the evidences of an existing Deity beneath his feet. In the merciful providence of a long-suffering God, the light of truth at length beamed upon his darkened understanding. In the winter of 1827, while engaged in his course of lectures in New York, an incident occurred which led him to a candid perusal of the New Testament. It was a visit to the death-bed of a Christian — the death-bed of a student of medicine. There he saw what reason could not explain nor philosophy fathom. He opened his Bible, and the secret was unfolded. He was in all things a seeker of the truth, and could not satisfy himself with any superficial examination.

He applied himself assiduously to the study of the New Testament; and that this sincere and thorough examination of the inspired volume was made the means of his full conversion, will best appear from his own eloquent pen. The following is an extract of a letter he addressed to a medical friend, Dr. Judson, a surgeon in the navy of the United States, who was at that time in the last stage of consumption:

"*Germantown, December 25th,* 1828.

In relation to dying, my dear friend, you talk like a sick man, and just as I used to do, when very despondent. Death is a debt we all owe to nature, and must eventually ensue from a mere wearing out of the machine, if not from disease. Nature certainly has a strong abhorrence to this cessation of corporeal action, and all animals have a dread of death who are conscious of its approach. A part of our dread of death is purely physical, and is avoidable only by a philosophical conviction of its necessity; but the greater part of our dread, and the terrors with which the avenues to the grave are surrounded, are from another and a more potent source. ''Tis conscience that makes cowards of us all,' and forces us by our terrors to confess, that we dread something beyond physical dissolution, and that we are terrified not at merely ceasing to breathe, but that we have not lived as we ought to have done, have not effected the good that was within the compass of our abilities, and neglected to exercise the talents we possessed, to the greatest advantage. The only remedy for this fear of death is to be sought by approaching the Author of all things in the way prescribed by himself, and not according to our own foolish imaginations. Humiliation of pride, denial of self, subjection of evil tempers and dispositions, and an entire submission to His will for support and direction, are the best preparatives for such an approach. A perusal of the gospels, in a spirit of real inquiry after a direction how to act, will certainly teach the way. In these gospels the Saviour himself has preached His own doctrines, and he who runs may read. He has prescribed the course; He shows how the approval and mercy of God may be won; He shows how awfully corrupt is man's nature, and how deadly his pride and stubbornness of heart, which cause him to try every subterfuge to avoid the humiliating confession of his own weakness, ignorance, and folly. But the same blessed Hand has stripped death of all the terrors which brooded around the grave, and converted the gloomy receptacle of our mortal remains into the portal of life and light. Oh! let me die the death of the righteous; let my last end and future state be like his!

This is all I know on the subject. I am no theologian, and have as great an aversion to priestcraft as one can entertain. I was once an infidel, as I told you in the West Indies. I became a Christian from conviction produced by the candid inquiry recommended to you. I know of no other way in which death can be stripped of its terrors; certainly none better can be wished. Philosophy is a fool, and pride a madman. Many persons die with what is called *manly firmness;* that is, having acted a part all their lives, according to their prideful creed, they must die *game*. They put on as smooth a face as they can, to impose on the spectators, and die *firmly*. But this is all deception: the true state of their minds at the very time, nine times out of ten, is worse than the most horrible imaginings even of hell itself. Some who have led lives adapted to sear their conscience and petrify all the moral sensibilities, die with a kind of indifference similar to that with which a hardened convict submits to a new infliction of disgraceful punishment. But the man who dies as a man ought to die, is the humble-minded, believing Christian; one who has tasted and enjoyed all the blessings of creation; who has had an enlightened view of the wisdom and glory of his Creator; who has felt the vanity of merely worldly pursuits and motives, and been permitted to know the mercies of a blessed Redeemer, as he approaches the narrow house appointed for all the living. Physical death may cause his senses to shrink and fail at the trial; but his mind, sustained by the Rock of Ages, is serene and unwavering. He relies not on his own righteousness, for that would be vain; but the arms of mercy are beneath him, the ministering spirits of the Omnipotent are around him. He does not die manfully, but he rests in Jesus; he blesses his friends, he casts his hope on One all-powerful to sustain and mighty to save, then sleeps in peace. He is dead, but liveth; for He who is the resurrection and the life has declared, 'Whoso believeth on me, though he were dead, yet shall he live.' 'And whosoever liveth and believeth in me, shall never die.'" . . . . .

This letter, which so truly contrasts the death-bed scene of the infidel with that of the Christian, so beautifully portrays the history of the change which had been effected in Dr. Godman's own sentiments and affections, and so clearly points the benighted wanderer to the true source of life and light, was not lost upon his friend to whom it was addressed. It described his condition, and it reached his heart.

Dr. Judson, though religiously instructed when young, having a pious clergyman for his father, and another for his elder brother, had nevertheless long since freed himself from what he called the prejudices of education, the shackles of priestcraft, and was ranging the fields of infidelity. He had acquired wealth and reputation, and was an estimable man in all the domestic relations of life; but the self-denying doctrines of the Saviour were too humbling to his proud spirit, and he could not submit to their influence. At the time he received Dr. Godman's letter, however, he was gloomy and despondent, looking forward with fearful forebodings to the period of his dissolution, which seemed not far distant. He had no confidence but that of the sceptic —no hope but that of ceasing to be. Aware of the fatal nature of the disease under which he had lingered for years, he had long been arming himself to meet the king of terrors with composure, that he might die like a philosopher, "*with manly firmness;*" but as he drew nearer to the grave, the clouds and darkness thickened around him, and he began to fear that there might be something beyond this narrow prison. His infidelity now began to give way, and he inquired with solicitude: "Is there such a thing as the new birth, and if so, in what does it consist?" He at length consented to make the investigation recommended by Dr. Godman. He took up the New Testament, and read it in the spirit of candid inquiry. A conviction of the truth of its doctrines fastened upon him. The clouds which had so long enveloped him were dissipated, light broke in upon his mind, and he was enabled to lay hold of the promises. The remaining days of his life were devoted to fervent prayer and the constant study of the Scriptures. Through the holy influences of Divine grace, he was enabled to rely with undoubting confidence on the infinite merits of his Redeemer, his soul was filled with heavenly composure, and the last words he uttered were, "Peace, peace." If he did not die with "*manly firmness*," he "*rested in Jesus*."

Dr. Godman's views of the authenticity and practical tendency of the gospel, are expressed with singular force and beauty in the following extract from an essay written not long before his death:

"Is proof wanting that these gospels are true? It is only necessary for an honest mind to read them candidly, to be convinced. Every occurrence is stated clearly, simply, and unostentatiously. The narrations are not supported by asseverations of their truth, nor by parade of witnesses: the circumstances described took place in presence of vast multitudes, and are told in that downright, unpretending manner which would have called forth innumerable positive contradictions had they been untrue. Mysteries are stated without attempt at explanation, because *explanation* is not necessary to establish the *existence* of facts, however mysterious. Miracles, also, attested by the presence of vast numbers, are stated in the plainest language of narration, in which the slightest working of imagination cannot be traced. This very simplicity, this unaffected sincerity, and quiet affirmation, have more force than a thousand witnesses—more efficacy than volumes of ambitious effort to support truth by dint of argumentation.

What motive could the evangelists have to falsify? The Christian kingdom is not *of this world*, nor *in it.* Christianity teaches disregard of its vanities, depreciates its honours and enjoyments, and sternly declares that none can be Christians but those who escape from its vices and allurements. There is no call directed to ambition, no gratification proposed to vanity: the sacrifice of self, the denial of all the propensities which relate to the gratification of passion or pride, with the most humble dependence upon God, are invariably taught and most solemnly enjoined, under penalty of the most awful consequences. Is it, then, wonderful that such a system should find revilers? Is it surprising that sceptics should abound, when the slightest allowance of belief would force them to condemn all their actions? Or is it to be wondered at that a purity of life and conversation so repugnant to human passions, and a humility so offensive to human pride, should be opposed, rejected, and contemned? Such is the true secret of the opposition to *religion*—such the cause inducing men who lead unchristian lives, to array the frailties, errors, weaknesses, and vices of individuals or sects, against *Christianity*, hoping to weaken or destroy the system by rendering ridiculous or contemptible those who *profess* to be governed by its influence, though their conduct shows them to be acting under an opposite spirit.

What is the mode in which this most extraordinary doctrine of Christianity is to be diffused? By force, temporal power, temporal rewards, earthly triumphs? None of these. By earnest persuasion, gentle entreaty, brotherly monition, paternal remonstrance. The dread resort of threatened punishment comes last; exhibited in sorrow, not in anger; told as a fearful truth, not denounced with vindictive exultation; while to the last moment the beamy shield of mercy is ready to be interposed for the saving of the endangered.

Human doctrines are wavering and mutable; the doctrines of the blessed and adorable Jesus, our Saviour, are fixed and immutable. The traditions of men are dissimilar and inconsistent; the declarations of the gospel are harmonious, not only with each other, but with the acknowledged attributes of the Deity, and the well-known condition of human nature.

What do sceptics propose to give us in exchange for this system of Christianity, with its 'hidden mysteries,' 'miracles,' 'signs and wonders?' Doubt, confusion, obscurity, annihilation! Life, without higher motive than selfishness; death, without hope! Is it for this that their zeal is so warmly displayed in proselyting? Is such the gain to accrue for the relinquishment of our souls? In very deed, this is the utmost they have to propose; and we can only account for their rancorous efforts to render others like themselves, by reflecting that misery loves company."

His intellect was strong and undimmed to the last, and almost the only change that could be observed in his mind was that which belongs to a being on the verge of eternity, in whose estimate the concerns of this life are sinking in comparison with the greater interests of that to which he is approaching. His principal delight was in the promises and consolations of the Bible, which was his constant companion. On one occasion, a few days before his death, while reading aloud from the New Testament to his family, his voice faltered, and he was desired to read no longer, as it appeared to oppress him. "It is not that," replied he; "but I feel so in the immediate presence of my Maker, that I cannot control my emotion!" In a manuscript volume which he sent to a friend, and which he intended to fill with original pieces of his own composition, he wrote as follows: "Did I not in all things feel most thoroughly convinced that the overruling of our plans by an all-wise Providence is always for good, I might regret that a part of my plan cannot be executed.

This was to relate a few curious incidents from among the events of my most singularly guided life, which, in addition to mere novelty or peculiarity of character, could not have failed practically to illustrate the importance of inculcating correct religious and moral principles, and imbuing the mind therewith from the very earliest dawn of intellect, from the very moment that the utter imbecility of infancy begins to disappear. May His holy will be done, who can raise up abler advocates to support the truth." "This is my first attempt to write in my Token; why may it not be the last? Oh! should it be, believe me, that the will of God will be most acceptable. Notwithstanding the life of neglect, sinfulness, and perversion of heart which I so long led, before it pleased Him to dash all my idols in the dust, I feel a humble hope in the boundless mercy of our blessed Lord and Saviour, who alone can save the soul from merited condemnation. May it be in the power of those who chance to read these lines, to say, Into thy hands I commit my spirit, for Thou hast redeemed me, O Lord! thou God of Truth!"

A reliance on the mercies of God through Jesus Christ became indeed the habitual frame of his mind, and imparted to the closing scenes of his life a solemnity and a calmness, a sweet serenity and a holy resignation, which robbed death of its sting and the grave of its victory. The following extracts from some of his letters afford additional evidence of the great and glorious change which he had been permitted to experience.

"*Philadelphia, Feb. 17th*, 1829.

MY DEAR FRIEND,—Since my last to you my health has suffered various and most afflicting changes."—"But thanks to the mercies of Him who is alone able to save, the valley and shadow of death were stripped of their terrors, and the descent to the grave was smoothed before me. Relying on the mercies and infinite merits of the Saviour, had it pleased God to call me then, I believe I should have died in a peaceful, humble confidence. But I have been restored to a state of comparative health, perhaps nearly to the condition in which I was when I wrote to Dr. Judson; and I am again allowed to think of the education of my children and the support of my family."

In reply to a letter from Professor Sewall, giving an account of the last moments of his friend Dr. Judson, he responds in the following feeling manner:

"*Germantown, May 21st*, 1829.

MY DEAR FRIEND,—I feel very grateful for your attention in sending me an account of our dear Judson's last moments. After all his doubts, difficulties, and mental conflicts, to know that the Father of mercies was pleased to open his eyes to the truth, and shed abroad in his heart the love and salvation offered through the Redeemer, is to me a source of the purest gratification, and a cause of the most sincere rejoicing. The bare possibility of my having been even slightly instrumental in effecting the blessed change of mind he experienced, excites in me emotions of gratitude to the Source of all good which words cannot express." — "My health has been in a very poor condition since my last to you. The warm weather now appears to have set in, and possibly I may improve a little, otherwise it will not be long before I follow our lately departed friend. Let me participate in the prayers you offer for the sick and afflicted, and may God grant me strength to die to His honour and glory, in the hopes and constancy derived from the merits and atonement of the blessed Saviour."

"*Philadelphia, Oct. 6th,* 1829.

MY DEAR FRIEND, — My health is, as for a considerable time past, in a very tolerable condition; that is, I can sit up a great part of the day, writing or reading, without much injury. My emaciation is great, and, though not very rapid, is steady, so that the change in my strength takes place almost imperceptibly. On the whole, though I suffer greatly, compared with persons in health, yet so gently have the chastenings of the Lord fallen upon me, that I am hourly called upon for thankfulness and gratitude for His unfailing mercies. Equal cause have I had for rejoicing, that I have learned to put my whole trust in Him, as He has raised me up help and friends in circumstances which seemed to render even hope impossible, and has blessed me and mine with peace and content in the midst of all afflictions, trials, and adversity."

In his last letter to Dr. Best, of Cincinnati, with whom he had long maintained an affectionate correspondence, he writes:

"It gives me great happiness to learn that you have been taught, as well as myself, to fly to the Rock of Ages for shelter against the afflictions of this life, and for hopes of eternal salvation. But for the hopes afforded me by an humble reliance on the all-sufficient atonement of our blessed Redeemer, I should have been the most wretched of men. But I trust that the afflictions I have endured have been sanctified to my awakening, and to the regeneration of my heart and life. May we, my dear friend, persist to cling to the only sure support against all that is evil in life and all that is fearful in death!"

Dr. Best's circumstances were in several respects similar to those of his friend Godman: like him, he had been a disbeliever in the Christian religion, and like him had been brought by a careful examination of its evidences to a perception and an acknowledgment of the truth. He too was at this time languishing in consumption, which brought him to the grave a few months after Dr. Godman; and like him he was supported and animated by the precious faith of the gospel, and yielded up his spirit in hope and peace.

Professor Sewall,* from whose account much of this memoir has been derived, remarks: "In the

* "An Introductory Lecture delivered November 1st, 1830, by Thomas Sewall, M. D., Professor of Anatomy and Physiology in the Columbian College, District of Columbia."

last letter which I ever received from him, he observes: 'I have just concluded the publication of the translation of Levasseur's account of Lafayette's progress through the United States, which will appear next week. My health has for the last week or two been very good, for me, since, notwithstanding my rather excessive application during this time, I continue to do well. My cough and expectoration are sufficiently troublesome; but by light diet, and avoiding all irritation, I have but very little trouble from night sweats, and generally sleep tolerably well. To-morrow I must resume my pen to complete some articles of zoology for the Encyclopedia Americana, now preparing in Boston. It shall be my constant endeavour to husband my strength to the last; and, by doing as much as is consistent with safety for the good of my fellow-creatures, endeavour to discharge a mite of the immense debt I owe for the never-failing bounties of Providence.' "

He did husband his strength, and he toiled with his pen almost to the last hours of his life; and by thus doing has furnished us with a singular evidence of the possibility of uniting the highest attainments in science, and the most ardent devotion to letters, with the firmest belief and the purest practice of the Christian. But the period of his dissolution was not distant: the summons arrived; and conscious that the messenger, who had been long in waiting, could not be bribed to tarry, he commended his little family in a fervent prayer to Him who has promised to be the 'Father of the fatherless, and the widow's God,' and then, with uplifted eyes and hands, and a face beaming with joy and confidence, resigned his spirit into the arms of his Redeemer, on the morning of the 17th of Fourth month, 1830.

A friend who was his constant companion during his sickness, and witnessed his last moments, writes thus:

"You ask me to give you an account of his last moments: they were such as have robbed me of all terror of death, and will afford me lasting comfort through life. The same self-composure and entire resignation which were so remarkable through his whole sickness, supported him to the end. Oh! it was not death; it was a release from mortal misery to everlasting happiness. Such calmness, when he prayed for us all—such a heavenly composure, even till the breath left him, you would have thought he was going only a short journey. During the day, his sufferings had been almost beyond enduring. Frequently did he pray that the Lord would give him patience to endure all till the end, knowing that it could not be many hours; and truly his prayers were heard. '*Lord Jesus, receive my soul,*' were the last words he uttered, and his countenance appeared as if he had a foretaste of heaven even before his spirit left this world."

The fine imagination and deep enthusiasm of Dr. Godman occasionally burst forth in impassioned poetry. He wrote verse and prose with almost equal facility, and had he lived and enjoyed leisure to prune the exuberance of his style, and to bestow the last polish upon his labours, he would have ranked as one of the great masters of our language, both in regard to the curious felicity and the strength and clearness of his diction. The following specimens of his poetical compositions are selected less for their intrinsic excellence, than for the picture which they furnish of his private meditations.

A MIDNIGHT MEDITATION.

"'Tis midnight's solemn hour! now wide unfurled
Darkness expands her mantle o'er the world;
The fire-fly's lamp has ceased its fitful gleam;
The cricket's chirp is hushed; the boding scream
Of the gray owl is stilled; the lofty trees
Scarce wave their summits to the failing breeze;
All nature is at rest, or seems to sleep;
'Tis thine alone, O man! to watch and weep!
Thine 'tis to feel thy system's sad decay,
As flares the taper of thy life away
Beneath the influence of fell disease:
Thine 'tis to *know* the want of mental ease
Springing from memory of time misspent,
Of slighted blessings, deepest discontent
And riotous rebellion 'gainst the laws
Of health, truth, heaven, to win the world's applause!

—Such was thy course, Eugenio; such thy hardened heart,
Till mercy spoke, and death unsheathed the dart,
Twanged his unerring bow, and drove the steel
Too deep to be withdrawn, too wide the wound to heal,
Yet left of life a feebly glimmering ray,
Slowly to sink and gently ebb away.

—And yet, how blest am I!
While myriad others lie
In agony of fever or of pain,
With parching tongue and burning eye,
Or fiercely throbbing brain;
My feeble frame, though spoiled of rest,
Is not of comfort dispossest.
My mind awake, looks up to Thee,
Father of mercy! whose blest hand I see
In all things acting for our good,
Howe'er thy mercies be misunderstood.

—See where the waning moon
Slowly surmounts yon dark tree-tops,
Her light increases steadily, and soon
The solemn night her stole of darkness drops:
Thus to my sinking soul, in hours of gloom,
The cheering beams of hope resplendent come,
Thus the thick clouds which sin and sorrow rear
Are changed to brightness, or swift disappear.

Hark! that shrill note proclaims approaching day;
The distant east is streaked with lines of gray;
Faint warblings from the neighbouring groves arise,
The tuneful tribes salute the brightening skies,
Peace breathes around; dim visions o'er me creep,
The weary night outwatched, thank God! I too may sleep.

LINES WRITTEN UNDER A FEELING OF THE IMMEDIATE APPROACH OF DEATH.

The damps of death are on my brow,
The chill is in my heart,
My blood has almost ceased to flow,
My hopes of life depart;
The valley and the shadow before me open wide,
But thou, O Lord! even there wilt be my guardian and my guide,

For what is pain, if Thou art nigh its bitterness to quell?
And where death's boasted victory, his last triumphant spell?
O Saviour! in that hour when mortal strength is nought,
When nature's agony comes on, and every anguished thought
Springs in the breaking heart a source of darkest woe,
Be nigh unto my soul, nor permit the floods o'erflow.
To Thee, to Thee alone! dare I raise my dying eyes;
Thou didst for all atone, by Thy wondrous sacrifice;
Oh! in Thy mercy's richness, extend Thy smiles on me,
And let my soul outspeak Thy praise, throughout eternity!"

Beneath the above stanzas, in the manuscript alluded to, is the following note: "Rather more than a year has elapsed since the above was first written. Death is now certainly nearer at hand; but my sentiments remain unchanged, except that my reliance on the Saviour is stronger."

It was a melancholy sight to witness the premature extinction of such a spirit; yet the dying couch on which genius, and virtue, and learning thus lay prostrated, beamed with more hallowed lustre, and taught a more salutary lesson, than could have been imparted by the proudest triumphs of intellect. The memory of Dr. Godman, his blighted promise and his unfinished labours, will long continue to call forth the vain regrets of men of science and learning. There are those who treasure up in their hearts, as a more precious recollection, his humble faith and his triumphant death, and who can meet with an eye of pity the scornful glance of the scoffer and the infidel, at being told that if Dr. Godman was a philosopher, he was also a Christian.

RAMBLES OF A NATURALIST.

RAMBLES OF A NATURALIST.

No. I.

FROM early youth devoted to the study of nature, it has always been my habit to embrace every opportunity of increasing my knowledge and pleasures by actual observation, and have ever found ample means of gratifying this disposition, wherever my place has been allotted by Providence. When an inhabitant of the country, it was sufficient to go a few steps from the door, to be in the midst of numerous interesting objects; when a resident of the crowded city, a healthful walk of half an hour placed me where my favourite enjoyment was offered in abundance; and now, when no longer able to seek in fields and woods and running streams for that knowledge which cannot readily be elsewhere obtained, the recollection of my former rambles is productive of a satisfaction which past pleasures but seldom bestow. Perhaps a statement of the manner in which my studies were pursued, may prove interesting to those who love the works of nature, and may not be aware how great a field for original observation is within their reach, or how vast a variety of instructive objects are easily accessible, even to the occupants of a bustling metropolis. To me it will be a source of great delight to spread these resources before the reader, and enable him so cheaply to participate in the pleasures I have enjoyed, as well as place him in the way of enlarging the general stock of knowledge, by communicating the results of his original observations.

One of my favourite walks was through Turner's Lane, which is about a quarter of a mile long, and not much wider than an ordinary street, being closely fenced in on both sides; yet my reader may feel surprised when informed that I found ample employment for all my leisure, during six weeks, within and about its precincts. On entering the lane from the Ridge road, I observed a gentle elevation of the turf beneath the lower rails of the fence, which appeared to be uninterruptedly continuous; and when I had cut through the verdant roof with my knife, it proved to be a regularly arched gallery or subterranean road, along which the inhabitants could securely travel at all hours, without fear of discovery. The sides and bottom of this arched way were smooth and clean, as if much used; and the raised superior portion had long been firmly consolidated by the grass roots, intermixed with tenacious clay. At irregular and frequently distant intervals, a side path diverged into the neighbouring fields, and, by its superficial situation, irregularity, and frequent openings, showed that its purpose was temporary, or had been only opened for the sake of procuring food. Occasionally I found a little gallery diverging from the main route beneath the fence, towards the road, and finally opening on the grass, as if the inmate had come out in the morning to breathe the early air, or to drink of the crystal dew which daily gemmed the close-cropped verdure. How I longed to detect the animal which tenanted these galleries, in the performance of his labours! Farther on, upon the top of a high bank, which prevented the pathway from continuing near the fence, appeared another evidence of the industry of my yet unknown miner. Half-a-dozen hillocks of loose, almost pulverised earth were thrown up, at irregular distances, communicating with the main gallery by side passages. Opening one of these carefully, it appeared to differ little from the common gallery in size, but it was very difficult to ascertain where the loose earth came from, nor have I ever been able to tell, since I never witnessed the formation of these hillocks, and conjectures are forbidden, where nothing but observation is requisite to the decision. My farther progress was now interrupted by a delightful brook which sparkled across the road, over a clear sandy bed; and here my little galleries turned into the field, coursing along at a moderate distance from the stream. I crept through the fence into the meadow on the west side, intending to discover, if possible, the animal whose works had first fixed my attention, but as I approached the bank of the rivulet, something suddenly retreated towards the grass, seeming to vanish almost unaccountably from sight. Very carefully examining the point at which it disappeared, I found the entrance of another gallery or burrow, but of very different construction from that first observed. This new one was formed in the grass, near and among whose roots and lower stems a small but regular covered way was practised. Endless, however, would have been the attempt to follow this, as it opened in various directions, and ran irregularly into the field, and towards the brook, by a great variety of passages. It evidently belonged to an animal totally different from the owner of the subterranean passage, as I subsequently discovered, and may hereafter relate. Tired of my unavailing pursuit, I now returned to the little brook, and seating myself on a stone, remained for some time unconsciously gazing on the fluid which gushed along in unsullied brightness over its pebbly bed. Opposite to my seat was an irregular hole in the bed of the stream, into which, in an idle mood, I pushed a small pebble with the end of my stick. What was my surprise, in a few seconds afterwards, to observe the water in this hole in motion, and the pebble I had pushed into it gently approaching the surface. Such was the fact: the hole was the dwelling of a stout little crayfish, or fresh-water lobster, who did not choose to be incommoded by the pebble, though doubtless he attributed its sudden arrival to the usual accidents of the stream, and not to my thoughtless movements. He had thrust his broad lobster-like claws under the stone, and then drawn them near to his mouth, thus making a kind of shelf; and, as he reached the edge of the hole, he suddenly extended his claws, and rejected the incumbrance from the lower side, or down stream. Delighted to have found a living object with whose habits I was unacquainted, I should have repeated my experiment, but the crayfish presently returned with what might be called an armful of rubbish, and threw it over the side of his cell, and down the stream, as before. Having watched him for some time while thus engaged, my attention was caught by the considerable number of similar holes along the margin and in the bed of the stream. One of these I explored with a small rod, and found it to be eight or ten inches deep, and widened below into a considerable chamber, in which the little lobster found a comfortable abode. Like all of his tribe, the crayfish makes considerable opposition to being removed from his dwelling, and bit smartly at the stick with his claws: as my present object was only to gain acquaintance with his dwelling, he was speedily permitted to return to it in peace. Under the end of a stone lying in the bed of the stream, something was floating in the pure current, which at first seemed like the tail of a fish; and being desirous to obtain a better view, I gently raised the stone on its edge, and was rewarded by a very beautiful sight. The object first observed was the tail of a beautiful salamander, whose sides were of a pale straw colour, flecked with circlets of the richest crimson. Its long lizard-like body seemed to be semi-transparent, and its slender limbs appeared like mere productions of the skin. Not far distant, and near where the upper end of the stone had been, lay crouched, as if asleep, one of the most beautifully-coloured frogs I had ever beheld. Its body was slender compared with most frogs, and its skin covered with stripes of bright reddish-brown and grayish-green, in such a manner as to recall the beautiful markings of the tiger's hide; and, since the time alluded to, it has received the name of *Tigrina* from Leconte, its first scientific describer. How long I should have been content to gaze at these beautiful animals, as they lay basking in the living water, I know not, had not the intense heat made me feel the necessity of seeking a shade. It was now past twelve o'clock: I began to retrace my steps towards the city; and, without any particular object, moved along by the little galleries examined in the morning. I had advanced but a short distance, when I found the last place where I had broken open the gallery was *repaired.* The earth was perfectly fresh, and I had lost the chance of discovering the miner, while watching my new acquaintances in the stream. Hurrying onward, the same circumstance uniformly presented; the injuries were all efficiently repaired, and had evidently been very recently completed. Here was one point gained: it was ascertained that these galleries were still inhabited, and I hoped soon to become acquainted with the inmates. But at this time it appeared fruitless to delay longer, and I returned home, filled with anticipations of pleasure from the success of my future researches. These I shall relate on another occasion, if such narrations as the present be thought of sufficient interest to justify their presentation to the reader.

JOHN.

No. II.

On the day following my first related excursion, I started early in the morning, and was rewarded by one sight, which could not otherwise have been obtained, well worth the sacrifice of an hour or two of sleep. There may be persons who will smile contemptuously at the idea of a *man's* being delighted with such trifles; nevertheless, we are not inclined to envy such as disesteem the pure gratification afforded by these simple and easily accessible pleasures. As I crossed an open lot on my way to the lane, a succession of gossamer spider-webs, lightly suspended from various weeds and small shrubs, attracted my attention. The dew which had formed during the night was condensed upon this delicate lace, in globules of most resplendent brilliance, whose clear lustre pleased while it dazzled the sight. In comparison with the immaculate purity of these dew-drops, which reflected and refracted the morning light in beautiful rays, as the gossamer webs trembled in the breeze, how poor would appear the most invaluable diamonds that were ever obtained from Golconda or Brazil! How rich would any monarch be that could boast the possession of *one* such, as here glittered in thousands on every herb and spray! They are exhaled in an hour or two, and lost; yet they are almost daily offered to the delighted contemplation of the real lover of nature, who is ever happy to witness the beneficence of the great Creator, not less displayed in trivial circumstances, than in the most wonderful of His works.

No particular change was discoverable in the works of my little miners, except that all the places which had been a second time broken down, were again repaired, showing that the animal had passed between the times of my visit; and it may not be uninteresting to observe how the repair was effected. It appeared, when the animal arrived at the spot broken open or exposed to the air, that it changed its direction sufficiently downwards to raise enough of earth from the lower surface to fill up the opening; this of course slightly altered the direction of the gallery at this point, and though the earth thrown up was quite pulverulent, it was so nicely arched as to retain its place, and soon became consolidated. Having broken open a gallery where the turf was very close, and the soil tenacious, I was pleased to find the direction of the chamber somewhat changed: on digging farther with my clasp-knife, I found a very beautiful cell excavated in very tough clay, deeper than the common level of the gallery, and towards one side. This little lodging-room would probably have held a small melon, and was nicely arched all round. It was perfectly clear, and quite smooth, as if much used: to examine it fully, I was obliged to open it completely. (The next day, it was replaced by another, made a little farther to one side, exactly of the same kind: it was replaced a second time, but when broken up a third time, it was left in ruins.) As twelve o'clock approached, my solicitude to discover the little miner increased to a considerable degree: previous observation led me to believe that about that time his presence was to be expected. I had trodden down the gallery for some inches in a convenient place, and stood close by, in vigilant expectation. My wishes were speedily gratified: in a short time the flattened gallery began at one end to be raised to its former convexity, and the animal rapidly advanced. With a beating heart, I thrust the knife-blade down by the side of the rising earth, and quickly turned it over to one side, throwing my prize fairly into the sunshine. For an instant, he seemed motionless from surprise, when I caught and imprisoned him in my hat. It would be vain for me to attempt a description of my pleasure in having thus succeeded, small as was my conquest. I was delighted with the beauty of my captive's fur; with the admirable adaptation of his diggers, or broad rose-tinted hands; the wonderful strength of his fore-limbs, and the peculiar suitableness of his head and neck to the kind of life the Author of nature had designed him for. It was the shrew-mole, or *scalops canadensis*, whose history and peculiarities of structure are minutely related in the first volume of Godman's American Natural History. All my researches never enabled me to discover a nest, female, or young one of this species. All I ever caught were males, though this most probably was a mere accident. The breeding of the scalops is nearly all that is wanting to render our knowledge of it complete.

This little animal has eyes, though they are not discoverable during its living condition, nor are they of any use to it above ground. In running round a room (until it had perfectly learned where all the obstacles stood), it would uniformly strike hard against them with its snout, and then turn. It appeared to me as singular, that a creature which fed upon living earth-worms with all the greediness of a pig, would not destroy the larvæ or maggots of the flesh-fly. A shrew-mole lived for many weeks in my study, and made use of a gun-case, into which he squeezed himself, as a burrow. Frequently he would carry the meat he was fed with into his retreat; and, as it was warm weather, the flies deposited their eggs in the same place. An offensive odour led me to discover this circumstance, and I found a number of large larvæ, over which the shrew-mole passed without paying them any attention; nor would he, when hungry, accept of such food, though nothing could exceed the eager haste with which he seized and munched earthworms. Often, when engaged in observing him thus employed, have I thought of the stories told me, when a boy, of the manner in which snakes were destroyed by swine: his voracity readily exciting a recollection of one of these animals, and the poor worms writhing and twining about his jaws answering for the snakes. It would be tedious were

I to relate all my rambles undertaken with a view to gain a proper acquaintance with this creature, at all hours of the day, and late in the evening, before day-light, etc. etc.

Among other objects which served as an unfailing source of amusement, when resting from the fatigue of my walks, was the little inhabitant of the brook which is spoken of in the extract made from the "Journal of a Naturalist," in last week's Friend. These merry swimmers occupied every little sunny pool in the stream, apparently altogether engaged in sport. A circumstance (not adverted to in that extract) connected with these insects, gives them additional interest to a close observer — they are allied by their structure and nature to those nauseous vermin, the cimices, or *bed-bugs;* all of which, whether found infesting fruits or our dormitories, are distinguished by their disgusting odour. But their distant relatives, called by the boys the *water-witches* and *apple-smellers*, the gyrinus natator above alluded to, has a delightful smell, exactly similar to that of the richest, mellowest apple. This peculiarly pleasant smell frequently causes the idler many unavailing efforts to secure some of these creatures, whose activity in water renders their pursuit very difficult, though by no means so much so as that of some of the long-legged water-spiders, which walk the waters dry-shod, and evade the grasp with surprising ease and celerity. What purposes either of these races serve in the great economy of nature, has not yet been ascertained, and will scarcely be determined until our store of *facts* is far more extensive than at present. Other and still more remarkable inhabitants of the brook, at the same time, came within my notice, and afforded much gratification in the observation of their habits. The description of these we are obliged to defer for the present, as we have already occupied as much space as can be allowed to our humble sketches.

JOHN.

No. III.

In moving along the borders of the stream, we may observe, where the sand or mud is fine and settled, a sort of mark or cutting, as if an edged instrument had been drawn along, so as to leave behind it a track or groove. At one end of this line, by digging a little into the mud with the hand, you will generally discover a shell of considerable size, which is tenanted by a molluscous animal of singular construction. On some occasions, when the mud is washed off from the shell, you will be delighted to observe the beautifully regular dark lines with which its greenish smooth surface is marked. Other species are found in the same situations, which, externally, are rough and inelegant, but within are ornamented to a most admirable degree, presenting a smooth surface of the richest pink, crimson, or purple, to which we have nothing of equal elegance to compare it. If the mere shells of these creatures be thus splendid, what shall we say of their internal structure, which, when examined by the microscope, offers a succession of wonders? The beautiful apparatus for respiration, formed of a network regularly arranged, of the most exquisitely delicate texture; the foot, or organ by which the shell is moved forward through the mud or water, composed of an expanded spongy extremity, capable of assuming various figures to suit particular purposes, and governed by several strong muscles, that move it in different directions; the ovaries, filled with myriads, not of eggs, but of perfect shells, or complete little animals, which, though not larger than the point of a fine needle, yet, when examined by the microscope, exhibit all the peculiarities of conformation that belong to the parent; the mouth, embraced by the nervous ganglion, which may be considered as the animal's brain; the stomach, surrounded by the various processes of the liver, and the strongly acting but transparent heart, all excite admiration and gratify our curiosity. The puzzling question often presents itself to the inquirer: Why so much elaborateness of construction and such exquisite ornament as are common to most of these creatures, should be bestowed? Destined to pass their lives in and under the mud, possessed of no sense that we are acquainted with, except that of touch, what purpose can ornament serve in them? However much of vanity there may be in asking the question, there is no answer to be offered. We cannot suppose that the individuals have any power of admiring each other, and we know that the foot is the only part they protrude from their shell, and that the inside of the shell is covered by the membrane called the mantle. Similar remarks may be made relative to conchology at large: the most exquisitely beautiful forms, colours, and ornaments are lavished upon genera and species which exist only at immense depths in the ocean, or buried in the mud; nor can any one form a satisfactory idea of the object the great Author of nature had in view, in thus profusely beautifying creatures occupying so low a place in the scale of creation.

European naturalists have hitherto fallen into the strangest absurdities concerning the motion of the bivalved shells, which five minutes' observation of nature would have served them to correct. Thus, they describe the upper part of the shell as the *lower*, and the *hind* part as the front, and speak of them as moving along on their rounded convex surface, like a boat on its keel, instead of advancing with the edges or open part of the shell towards the earth. All these mistakes have been corrected, and the true mode of progression indicated from actual observation, by our fellow-citizen, Isaac Lea, whose recently published communications to the American Philosophical Society reflect the highest credit upon their author, who is a naturalist in the best sense of the term.

As I wandered slowly along the borders of the run, towards a little wood, my attention was caught by a considerable collection of shells lying near an old stump. Many of these appeared to have been recently emptied of their contents, and others seemed to have long remained exposed to the weather. On most of them, at the thinnest part of the edge, a peculiar kind of fracture was obvious, and this seemed to be the work of an animal. A closer examination of the locality showed the footsteps of a quadruped, which I readily believed to be the muskrat, more especially as, upon examining the adjacent banks, numerous traces of burrows were discoverable. It is not a little singular that this animal, unlike all others of the larger gnawers, as the beaver, etc. appears to increase instead of diminishing with the increase of population. Whether it is that the dams and other works thrown up by men afford more favourable situations for their multiplication, or their favourite food is found in greater abundance, they certainly are quite as numerous now, if not more so, than when the country was first discovered, and are to be found at this time almost within the limits of the city. By the construction of their teeth, as well as all the parts of the body, they are closely allied to the rat kind; though in size, and some peculiarities of habit, they more closely approximate the beaver. They resemble the rat, especially, in not being exclusively herbivorous, as is shown by their feeding on the uniones or muscles above mentioned. To obtain this food requires no small exertion of their strength; and they accomplish it by introducing the claws of their forepaws between the two edges of the shell, and tearing it open by main force. Whoever has tried to force open one of these shells, containing a living animal, may form an idea of the effort made by the muskrat: the strength of a strong man would be requisite to produce the same result in the same way.

The burrows of muskrats are very extensive, and consequently injurious to dykes and dams, meadow banks, etc. The entrance is always under water, and thence sloping upwards above the level of the water, so that the muskrat has to dive in going in and out. These creatures are excellent divers and swimmers, and, being nocturnal, are rarely seen unless by those who watch for them at night. Sometimes we alarm one near the mouth of the den, and he darts away across the water, near the bottom, marking his course by a turbid streak in the stream: occasionally we are made aware of the passage of one to some distance down the current, in the same way; but in both cases the action is so rapidly performed, that we should scarcely imagine what was the cause, if not previously informed. Except by burrowing into and spoiling the banks, they are not productive of much evil, their food consisting principally of the roots of aquatic plants, in addition to the shell-fish. The musky odour which gives rise to their common name is caused by glandular organs placed near the tail, filled with a viscid and powerfully musky fluid, whose uses we know but little of, though it is thought to be intended as a guide by which these creatures may discover each other. This inference is strengthened by finding some such contrivance in different races of animals, in various modifications. A great number carry it in pouches similar to those just mentioned. Some, as the musk animal, have the pouch under the belly; the shrew has the glands on the side; the camel on the back of the neck; the crocodile under the throat, etc. At least no other use has ever been assigned for this apparatus, and in all creatures possessing it the arrangement seems to be adapted peculiarly to the habits of the animals.

The crocodile, for instance, generally approaches the shore in such a manner as to apply the neck and throat to the soil, while the hinder part of the body is under water. The glands under the throat leave the traces of his presence, therefore, with ease, as they come into contact with the shore. The glandular apparatus on the back of the neck of the male camel, seems to have reference to the general elevation of the olfactory organs of the female; and the dorsal gland of the peccary, no doubt, has some similar relation to the peculiarities of the race.

The value of the fur of the muskrat causes many of them to be destroyed, which is easily enough effected by means of a trap. This is a simple box, formed of rough boards nailed together, about three feet long, having an iron door, made of pointed bars, opening *inwards*, at both ends of the box. This trap is placed with the end opposite to the entrance of a burrow observed during the day-time. In the night, when the muskrat sallies forth, he enters the box, instead of passing into the open air, and is drowned, as the box is quite filled with water. If the traps be visited and emptied during the night, two may be caught in each trap, as muskrats from other burrows may come to visit those where the traps are placed, and thus one be taken going in as well as one coming out. These animals are frequently very fat, and their flesh has a very wholesome appearance, and would probably prove good food. The musky odour, however, prejudices strongly against its use; and it is probable that the flesh is rank, as the muscles it feeds on are nauseous and bitter, and the roots which supply the rest of its food are generally unpleasant and acrid. Still, we should not hesitate to partake of its flesh, in case of necessity, especially if of a young animal, from which the musk-bag had been removed immediately after it was killed.

In this vicinity the muskrat does not build himself a house for the winter, as our fields and dykes are too often visited. But in other parts of the country, where extensive marshes exist, and muskrats are abundant, they build very snug and substantial houses, quite as serviceable and ingenious as those of the beaver. They do not dam the water as the beaver, nor cut branches of trees to serve for the walls of their dwellings. They make it of mud and rushes, raising a cone two or three feet high, having the entrance on the south side, under water. About the year 1804, I saw several of them in Worrell's marsh, near Chestertown, Maryland, which were pointed out to me by an old black man who made his living principally by trapping these animals for the sake of their skins. A few years since I visited the marshes near the mouth of Magerthy river, in Maryland, where I was informed, by a resident, that the muskrats still built regularly every winter. Perhaps these quadrupeds are as numerous in the vicinity of Philadelphia as elsewhere, as I have never examined a stream of fresh water, dyked meadow, or mill-dam, hereabout, without seeing traces of vast numbers. Along all the water-courses and meadows in Jersey, opposite Philadelphia, and in the meadows of the Neck, below the Navy-Yard, there must be large numbers of muskrats. Considering the value of the fur, and the ease and trifling expense at which they might be caught, we have often felt surprised that more of them are not taken, especially as we have so many poor men complaining of wanting something to do. By thinning the number of musk-rats, a positive benefit would be conferred on the farmers and furriers, to say nothing of the profits to the individual.

JOHN.

No. IV.

My next visit to my old hunting-ground, the lane and brook, happened on a day in the first hay-harvest, when the verdant sward of the meadows was rapidly sinking before the keen-edged scythes swung by vigorous mowers. This unexpected circumstance afforded me considerable pleasure, for it promised me a freer scope to my wanderings, and might also enable me to ascertain various particulars concerning which my curiosity had long been awakened. Nor was this promise unattended by fruition of my wishes. The reader may recollect that, in my first walk, a neat burrow in the grass, above ground, was observed, without my knowing its author. The advance of the mowers explained this satisfactorily, for in cutting the long grass, they exposed several nests of field-mice, which, by means of these grass-covered alleys, passed to the stream in search of food or drink, unseen by their enemies, the hawks and owls. The numbers of these little creatures were truly surprising: their fecundity is so great, and their food so abundant, that, were they not preyed upon by many other animals, and destroyed in great numbers by man, they would become exceedingly troublesome. There are various species of them, all bearing a very considerable resemblance to each other, and having, to an incidental observer, much of the appearance of the domestic mouse. Slight attention, however, is requisite to perceive very striking differences, and the discrimination of these will prove a source of considerable gratification to the inquirer. The nests are very nicely made, and look much like a bird's nest, being lined with soft materials, and usually placed in some snug little hollow, or at the root of a strong tuft of grass. Upon the grass roots and seeds these nibblers principally feed; and, where very abundant, the effects of their hunger may be seen in the brown and withered aspect of the grass they have injured at the root. But, under ordinary circumstances, the hawks, owls, domestic cat, weasels, crows, etc. keep them in such limits, as prevent them from doing essential damage.

I had just observed another and a smaller grassy covered way, where the mowers had passed along, when my attention was called towards a wagon at a short distance, which was receiving its load. Shouts and laughter, accompanied by a general running and scrambling of the people, indicated that some rare sport was going forward. When I approached, I found that the object of chase was a jumping mouse, whose actions it was truly delightful to witness. When not closely pressed by its pursuers, it ran with some rapidity, in the usual manner, as if seeking concealment. But in a moment it would vault into the air, and skim along for ten or twelve feet, looking more like a bird than a little quadruped. After continuing this for some time, and nearly exhausting its pursuers with running and falling over each other, the frightened creature was accidentally struck down by one of the workmen, during one of its beautiful leaps, and killed. As the hunters saw nothing worthy of attention in the dead body of the animal, they very willingly resigned it to me; and with great satisfaction I retreated to a willow shade, to read what nature had written in its form for my instruction. The general appearance was mouse-like; but the length and slenderness of the body, the shortness of its fore-limbs, and the disproportionate length of its hind-limbs, together with the peculiarity of its tail, all indicated its adaptation to the peculiar kind of action I had just witnessed. A sight of this little creature vaulting or bounding through the air, strongly reminded me of what I had read of the great kangaroo of New Holland; and I could not help regarding our little jumper as in some respects a sort of miniature resemblance of that curious animal. It was not evident, however, that the jumping mouse derived the aid from its tail, which so powerfully assists the kangaroo. Though long, and sufficiently stout in proportion, it had none of the robust muscularity which, in the New Holland animal, impels the lower part of the body immediately upward. In this mouse, the leap is principally, if not entirely, effected by a sudden and violent extension of the long hind-limbs, the muscles of which are strong, and admirably suited to their object. We have heard that these little animals feed on the roots, etc. of the green herbage, and that they are every season to be found in the meadows. It may perhaps puzzle some to imagine how they subsist through the severities of winter, when vegetation is at rest, and the earth generally frozen. Here we find another occasion to admire the all-perfect designs of the awful Author of nature, who has endowed a great number of animals with the faculty of retiring into the earth, and passing whole months in a state of repose so complete, as to allow all the functions of the body to be suspended, until the returning warmth of the spring calls them forth to renewed activity and enjoyment. The jumping mouse, when the chill weather begins to draw nigh, digs down about six or eight inches into the soil, and there forms a little globular cell, as much larger than his own body as will allow a sufficient covering of fine grass to be introduced. This being obtained, he contrives to coil up his body and limbs in the centre of the soft dry grass, so as to form a complete ball; and so compact is this, that, when taken out with the torpid animal, it may be rolled across a floor without injury. In this snug cell, which is soon filled up and closed externally, the jumping mouse securely abides through all the frosts and storms of winter, needing neither food nor fuel, being utterly quiescent, and apparently dead, though susceptible at any time of reanimation, by being very gradually stimulated by light and heat.

The little burrow under examination, when called to observe the jumping mouse, proved to be made by the merry musicians of the meadows, the field-crickets, *acheta campestris.* These lively black crickets are very numerous, and contribute very largely to that general song which is so delightful to the ear of the true lover of nature, as it rises on the air from myriads of happy creatures rejoicing amid the bounties conferred on them by Providence. It is not *a voice* that the crickets utter, but a regular vibration of musical chords, produced by nibbing the nervures of the elytra against a sort of network intended to produce the vibrations. The reader will find an excellent description of the apparatus in Kirby and Spence's book, but he may enjoy a much more satisfactory comprehension of the whole, by visiting the field-cricket in his summer residence, see him tuning his viol, and awakening the echoes with his music. By such an examination as may be there obtained, he may derive more knowledge than by frequent perusal of the most eloquent writings, and perhaps observe circumstances which the learned authors are utterly ignorant of.

Among the great variety of burrows formed in the grass, or under the surface of the soil, by various animals and insects, there is one that I have often anxiously and, as yet, fruitlessly explored. This burrow is formed by the smallest quadruped animal known to man, the minute *shrew,* which, when full grown, rarely exceeds the weight of *thirty-six grains.* I had seen specimens of this very interesting creature in the museum, and had been taught, by a more experienced friend, to distinguish its burrow, which I have often perseveringly traced, with the hope of finding the living animal, but in vain. On one occasion, I patiently pursued a burrow nearly round a large barn, opening it all the way. I followed it under the barn floor, which was sufficiently high to allow me to crawl beneath. There I traced it about to a tiresome extent, and was at length rewarded by discovering where it terminated, under a foundation-stone, perfectly safe from my attempts. Most probably a whole family of them were then present, and I had my labour for my pains. As these little creatures are nocturnal, and are rarely seen, from the nature of the places they frequent, the most probable mode of taking them alive would be, by placing a small mouse-trap in their way, baited with a little tainted or slightly spoiled meat. If a common mouse-trap be used, it is necessary to work it over with additional wire, as this shrew could pass between the bars even of a close mouse-trap. They are sometimes killed by cats, and thus obtained, as the cat never eats them, perhaps on account of their rank smell, owing to a peculiar glandular apparatus on each side, that pours out a powerfully odorous greasy substance. The species of the shrew genus are not all so exceedingly diminutive, as some of them are even larger than a common mouse. They have their teeth coloured at the tips in a remarkable manner; it is generally of a pitchy brown, or dark chestnut hue, and, like the colouring of the teeth in the beaver and other animals, is owing to the enamel being thus formed, and not to any mere accident of diet. The shrews are most common about stables and cow-houses; and there, should I ever take the field again, my traps shall be set, as my desire to have one of these little quadrupeds is still as great as ever.

JOHN.

No. V.

Hitherto my rambles have been confined to the neighbourhood of a single spot, with a view of showing how perfectly accessible to all, are numerous and various interesting natural objects. This habit of observing in the manner indicated, began many years anterior to my visit to the spots heretofore mentioned, and have extended through many parts of our own and another country. Henceforward my observations shall be presented without reference to particular places, or even of one place exclusively, but with a view to illustrate whatever may be the subject of description, by giving all I have observed of it under various circumstances.

A certain time of my life was spent in that part of Anne Arundel county, Md. which is washed by the river Patapsco on the north, the great Chesapeake bay on the west, and the Severn river on the south. It is in every direction cut up by creeks, or arms of the rivers and bay, into long, flat strips of land, called necks, the greater part of which is covered by dense pine-forests, or thickets of small shrubs and saplings, rendered impervious to human footsteps by the growth of vines, whose inextricable mazes nothing but a fox, wild-cat, or weasel could thread The soil cleared for cultivation is very generally poor, light, and sandy, though readily susceptible of improvement, and yielding a considerable produce in Indian corn and most of the early garden vegetables, by the raising of which for the Baltimore market the inhabitants obtain all their ready money. The blight of slavery has long extended its influence over this region, where all its usual effects are but too obviously visible. The white inhabitants are few in number, widely distant from each other; and manifest, in their mismanagement and half-indigent circumstances, how trifling an advantage they derive from the thraldom of their dozen or more of sturdy blacks, of different sexes and ages. The number of marshes formed at the heads of the creeks, render this country frightfully unhealthy in autumn, at which time the life of a resident physician is one of incessant toil and severe privation. Riding from morning till night, to get round to visit a few patients, his road leads generally through pine-forests, whose aged and lofty trees, encircled by a dense undergrowth, impart an air of sombre and unbroken solitude. Rarely or never does he encounter a white person on his way, and only once in a while will he see a miserably tattered negro, seated on a sack of corn, carried by a starveling horse or mule, which seems poorly able to bear the weight to the nearest mill. The red-head woodpecker and the flicker, or yellow-hammer, a kindred species, occasionally glance across his path; sometimes, when he turns his horse to drink at the dark-coloured branch (as such streams are locally called), he disturbs a solitary rufous-thrush engaged in washing its plumes; or, as he moves steadily along, he is slightly startled by a sudden appearance of the towhé bunting close to the side of the path. Except these creatures, and these by no means frequently seen, he rarely meets with animated objects: at a distance the harsh voice of the crow is often heard, or flocks of them are observed in the cleared fields, while now and then the buzzard, or turkey-vulture, may be seen wheeling in graceful circles in the higher regions of the air, sustained by his broadly-expanded wings, which apparently remain in a state of permanent and motionless extension. At other seasons of the year, the physician must be content to live in the most positive seclusion: the white people are all busily employed in going to and from market, and even were they at home, they are poorly suited for companionship. I here spent month after month, and, except the patients I visited, saw no one but the blacks: the house in which I boarded was kept by a widower, who, with myself, was the only white man within the distance of a mile or two. My only compensation was this—the house was pleasantly situated on the bank of Curtis's creek, a considerable arm of the Patapsco, which extended for a mile or two beyond us, and immediately in front of the door expanded so as to form a beautiful little bay. Of books I possessed very few, and those exclusively professional; but in this beautiful expanse of sparkling water, I had a book opened before me which a life-time would scarcely suffice me to read through. With the advantage of a small but neatly made and easily manageable skiff, I was always independent of the service of the blacks, which was ever repugnant to my feelings and principles. I could convey myself in whatever direction objects of inquiry might present, and as my little bark was visible for a mile in either direction from the house, a handkerchief waved, or the loud shout of a negro, was sufficient to recall me, in case my services were required.

During the spring months, and while the garden vegetables are yet too young to need a great deal of attention, the proprietors frequently employ their blacks in hauling the seine; and this in these creeks is productive of an ample supply of yellow perch, which affords a very valuable addition to the diet of all. The blacks in an especial manner profit by this period of plenty, since they are permitted to eat of them without restraint, which cannot be said of any other sort of provision allowed them. Even the pigs and crows obtain their share of the abundance, as the fishermen, after picking out the best fish, throw the smaller ones on the beach. But as the summer months approach, the aquatic grass begins to grow, and this fishing can no longer be continued, because the grass rolls the seine up in a wisp, so that it can contain nothing. At this time the spawning season of the different species of sun-fish begins, and to me this was a time of much gratification. Along the edge of the river, where the depth of water was not greater than from four feet to as shallow as twelve inches, an observer would discover a succession of circular spots cleared of the surrounding grass, and showing a clear sandy bed. These spots, or cleared spaces, we may regard as the nest of this beautiful fish. There, balanced in the transparent wave, at the distance of six or eight inches from the bottom, the sun-fish is suspended in the glittering sunshine, gently swaying its beautiful tail and fins; or, wheeling around in the limits of its little circle, appears to be engaged in keeping it clear of all incumbrances. Here the mother deposits her eggs or spawn, and never did hen guard her callow brood with more eager vigilance, than the sun-fish the little circle within which her promised offspring are deposited. If another individual approach too closely to her borders, with a fierce and angry air she darts against it, and forces it to retreat. Should any small and not too heavy object be dropped in the nest, it is examined with jealous attention, and displaced if the owner be not satisfied of its harmlessness. At the approach of man she flies with great velocity into deep water, as if willing to conceal that her presence was more than accidental where first seen. She may, after a few minutes, be seen cautiously venturing to return, which is at length done with volocity; then she would take a hurried turn or two around, and scud back again to the shady bowers formed by the river grass, which grows up from the bottom to within a few feet of the surface, and attains to twelve, fifteen, or more feet in length. Again she ventures forth from the depths; and, if no farther cause of fear presented, would gently sail into the placid circle of her home, and with obvious satisfaction explore it in every part.

Besides the absolute pleasure I derived from visiting the habitations of these glittering tenants of the river, hanging over them from my little skiff, and watching their every action, they frequently furnished me with a very acceptable addition to my frugal table. Situated as my boarding-house was, and all the inmates of the house busily occupied in raising vegetables to be sent to market, our bill of fare offered little other change than could be produced by varying the mode of cookery. It was either broiled bacon and potatoes, or fried bacon and potatoes, or cold bacon and potatoes, and so on at least six days out of seven. But, as soon as I became acquainted with the habits of the sun-fish, I procured a neat circular iron hoop for a net, secured to it a piece of an old seine, and whenever I desired to dine on *fresh* fish, it was only necessary to take my skiff, and push her gently along from one sun-fish nest to another, myriads of which might be seen along all the shore. The fish, of course, darted off as soon as the boat first drew near, and during this absence the net was placed so as to cover the nest, of the bottom of which the meshes but slightly intercepted the view. Finding all things quiet, and not being disturbed by the net, the fish would resume its central station, the net was suddenly raised, and the captive placed in the boat. In a quarter of an hour, I could generally take as many in this way as would serve two men for dinner; and when an acquaintance accidentally called to see me, during the season of sun-fish, it was always in my power to lessen our dependence on the endless bacon. I could also always select the finest and largest of these fish, as, while standing up in the boat, one could see a considerable number at once, and thus choose the best. Such was their abundance, that the next day would find all the nests reoccupied. Another circumstance connected with this matter gave me no small satisfaction: the poor blacks, who could rarely get time for angling, soon learned how to use my net with dexterity; and thus, in the ordinary time allowed them for dinner, would borrow it, run down to the shore, and catch some fish to add to their very moderate allowance.

JOHN.

No. VI.

After the sun-fish, as regular annual visitants of the small rivers and creeks containing salt or brackish water, came the crabs, in vast abundance, though for a very different purpose. These singularly-constructed and interesting beings furnished me with another excellent subject for observation; and, during the period of their visitation, my skiff was in daily requisition. Floating along with an almost imperceptible motion, a person looking from the shore might have supposed her entirely adrift; for, as I was stretched at full length across the seats, in order to bring my sight as close to the water as possible without inconvenience, no one would have observed my presence from a little distance. The crabs belong to a very extensive tribe of beings which carry their *skeletons* on the *outside* of their bodies, instead of within; and, of necessity, the fleshy, muscular, or moving power of the body is placed in a situation the reverse of what occurs in animals of a higher order, which have internal skeletons or solid frames to their systems. This peculiarity of the crustaceous animals, and various other beings, is attended with one apparent inconvenience—when they have grown large enough to fill their shell or skeleton completely, they cannot grow farther, because the skeleton, being external, is incapable of enlargement. To obviate this difficulty, the Author of nature has endowed them with the power of casting off the entire shell, increasing in size, and forming another equally hard and perfect, for several seasons successively, until the greatest or maximum size is attained, when the change or sloughing ceases to be necessary, though it is not always discontinued on that account. To undergo this change with greater ease and security, the crabs seek retired and peaceful waters, such as the beautiful creek I have been speaking of, whose clear, sandy shores are rarely disturbed by waves causing more than a pleasing murmur, and where the number of enemies must be far less, in proportion, than in the boisterous waters of the Chesapeake, their great place of concourse. From the first day of their arrival, in the latter part of June, until the time of their departure, which in this creek occurred towards the first of August, it was astonishing to witness the vast multitudes which flocked towards the head of the stream.

It is not until they have been for some time in the creek, that the moult or sloughing generally commences. They may be then observed gradually coming closer in shore, to where the sand is fine, fairly exposed to the sun, and a short distance farther out than the lowest water-mark, as they must always have at least a depth of three or four inches water upon them.

The individual having selected his place, becomes perfectly quiescent, and no change is observed, during some hours, but a sort of swelling along the edges of the great upper shell at its back part. After a time, this posterior edge of the shell becomes fairly disengaged, like the lid of a chest, and now the more difficult work of withdrawing the great claws from their cases, which every one recollects to be vastly larger at their extremities and between the joints than the joints themselves. A still greater apparent difficulty presents in the shedding of the sort of tendon which is placed within the muscles. Nevertheless, the Author of nature has adapted them to the accomplishment of all this. The disproportionate sized claws undergo a peculiar softening, which enables the crab, by a very steadily continued, scarcely perceptible effort, to pull them out of their shells, and the business is completed by the separation of the complex parts about the mouth and eyes. The crab now slips out from the slough, settling near it on the sand. It is now covered by a soft, perfectly flexible skin; and, though possessing precisely the same form as before, seems incapable of the slightest exertion. Notwithstanding that such is its condition, while you are gazing on this helpless creature, it is sinking in the fine loose sand, and in a short time is covered up sufficiently to escape the observation of careless or inexperienced observers. Neither can one say how this is effected, although it occurs under their immediate observation; the motions employed to produce the displacement of the sand are too slight to be appreciated, though it is most probably owing to a gradual lateral motion of the body, by which the sand is displaced in the centre beneath, and thus gradually forced up at the sides until it falls over and covers the crab. Examine him within twelve hours, and you will find the skin becoming about as hard as fine writing-paper, producing a similar crackling if compressed; twelve hours later, the shell is sufficiently stiffened to require some slight force to bend it, and the crab is said to be in *buckram*, as in the first stage it was in *paper*. It is still helpless, and offers no resistance; but, at the end of thirty-six hours, it shows that its natural instincts are in action, and, by the time forty-eight hours have elapsed, the crab is restored to the exercise of all his functions. I have stated the above as the periods in which the stages of the moult are accomplished, but I have often observed that the rapidity of this process is very much dependent upon the temperature, and especially upon sunshine. A cold, cloudy, raw, and disagreeable spell happening at this period, though by no means common, will retard the operation considerably, protracting the period of helplessness. This is the harvest season of the white fisherman and of the poor slave. The laziest of the former are now in full activity, wading along the shore from morning till night, dragging a small boat after them, and holding in the other hand a forked stick, with which they raise the crabs from the sand. The period during which the crabs remain in the paper state is so short, that great activity is required to gather a sufficient number to take to market, but the price at which they are sold is sufficient to awaken all the cupidity of the crabbers. Two dollars a dozen is by no means an uncommon price for them, when the season first comes on: they subsequently come down to a dollar, and even to fifty cents, at any of which rates the trouble of collecting them is well paid. The slaves search for them at night, and then are obliged to kindle a fire of pine-knots on the bow of the boat, which strongly illuminates the surrounding water, and enables them to discover the crabs. Soft crabs are, with great propriety, regarded as an exquisite treat by those who are fond of such eating; and though many persons are unable to use crabs or lobsters in any form, there are few who taste of the soft crabs without being willing to recur to them. As an article of luxury, they are scarcely known north of the Chesapeake, though there is nothing to prevent them from being used to a considerable extent in Philadelphia, especially since the opening of the Chesapeake and Delaware canal. During the last summer, I had the finest soft crabs from Baltimore. They arrived at the market in the afternoon, were fried according to rule, and placed in a tin butter-kettle, then covered for an inch or two with melted lard, and put on board the steam-boat which left Baltimore at five o'clock the same afternoon. The next morning before ten o'clock they were in Philadelphia, and at one they were served up at dinner in Germantown. The only difficulty in the way is that of having persons to attend to their procuring and transmission, as, when cooked directly after they arrive at market, and forwarded with as little delay as above mentioned, there is no danger of their being the least injured.

At other seasons, when the crabs did not come close to the shore, I derived much amusement by taking them in the deep water. This is always easily effected by the aid of proper bait: a leg of chicken, piece of any raw meat, or a salted or spoiled herring, tied to a twine string of sufficient length, and a hand net of convenient size, is all that is necessary. You throw out your line and bait, or you fix as many lines to your boat as you please, and in a short time you see, by the straightening of the line, that the bait has been seized by a crab, who is trying to make off with it. You then place your net where it can conveniently be picked up, and commence steadily but gently to draw in your line, until you have brought the crab sufficiently near the surface to distinguish him: if you draw him nearer, he will see you, and immediately let go; otherwise, his greediness and voracity will make him cling to his prey to the last. Holding the line in the left hand, you now dip your net edge foremost into the water at some distance from the line, carry it down perpendicularly until it is five or six inches lower than the crab, and then with a sudden turn bring it directly before him, and lift up at the same time. Your prize is generally secured, if your net be at all properly placed; for, as soon as he is alarmed, he pushes directly downwards, and is received in the bag of the net. It is better to have a little water in the bottom of the boat, to throw them into, as they are easier emptied out of the net, always letting go when held over the water. This a good crabber never forgets, and should he unluckily be seized by a large crab, he holds him over the water, and is freed at once, though he loses his game. When not held over the water, they bite sometimes with dreadful obstinacy; and I have seen it necessary to crush the forceps or claws before one could be induced to let go the fingers of a boy. A poor black fellow also placed himself in an awkward situation — the crab seized him by a finger of his right hand, but he was unwilling to lose his captive by holding him over the water; instead of which, he attempted to secure the other claw with his left hand, while he tried to crush the biting claw between his teeth. In doing this, he somehow relaxed his left hand, and with the other claw the crab seized poor Jem by his under lip, which was by no means a thin one, and forced him to roar with pain. With some difficulty he was freed from his tormentor, but it was several days before he ceased to excite laughter, as the severe bite was followed by a swelling of the lip, which imparted a most ludicrous expression to a naturally comical countenance.

JOHN.

No. VII.

On the first arrival of the crabs, when they throng the shoals of the creeks in vast crowds, as heretofore mentioned, a very summary way of taking them is resorted to by the country people, and for a purpose that few would suspect, without having witnessed it. They use a three-pronged fork or gig, made for this sport, attached to a long handle; the crabber, standing up in the skiff, pushes it along until he is over a large collection of crabs, and then strikes his spear among them. By this several are transfixed at once, and lifted into the boat, and the operation is repeated until enough have been taken. The purpose to which they are to be applied is to feed the hogs, which very soon learn to collect in waiting upon the beach, when the crab spearing is going on. Although these bristly gentry appear to devour almost all sorts of food with great relish, it seemed to me that they regarded the crabs as a most luxurious banquet; and it was truly amusing to see the grunters, when the crabs were thrown on shore for them, and were scampering off in various directions, seizing them in spite of their threatening claws, holding them down with one foot, and speedily reducing them to a state of helplessness by breaking off their forceps. Such a crunching and cracking of the unfortunate crabs I never have witnessed since; and I might have commiserated them more, had not I known that death in some form or other was continually awaiting them, and that their devourers were all destined to meet their fate in a few months in the stye, and thence through the smoke-house to be placed upon our table. On the shores of the Chesapeake I have caught crabs in a way commonly employed by all those who are unprovided with boats and nets. This is to have a forked stick and a baited line, with which the crabber wades out as far as he thinks fit, and then throws out his line. As soon as he finds he has a bite, he draws the line in, cautiously lifting but a very little from the bottom. As soon as it is near enough to be fairly in reach, he quickly, yet with as little movement as possible, secures the crab by placing the forked stick across his body, and pressing him against the sand. He must then stoop down and take hold of the crab by the two posterior swimming legs, so as to avoid being seized by the claws. Should he not wish to carry each crab ashore as he catches it, he pinions or *spansels* (as the fishermen call it) them. This is a very effectual mode of disabling them from using their biting claws, yet it is certainly not the most humane operation: it is done by taking the first of the sharp-pointed feet of each side, and forcing it in for the length of the joint behind the moveable joint or thumb of the opposite biting claw. The crabs are then strung upon a string or wythe, and allowed to hang in the water until the crabber desists from his occupations. In the previous article, crabs were spoken of as curious and interesting, and the reader may not consider the particulars thus far given as being particularly so. Perhaps, when he takes them altogether, he will agree that they have as much that is curious about their construction as almost any animal we have mentioned, and in the interesting details we have as yet made but a single step.

The circumstance of the external skeleton has been mentioned; but who would expect an animal as low in the scale as a crab, to be furnished with ten or twelve pair of jaws to its mouth? Yet such is the fact; and all these variously-constructed pieces are provided with appropriate muscles, and move in a manner which can scarcely be explained, though it may be very readily comprehended when once observed in living nature. But, after all the complexity of the jaws, where would an inexperienced person look for their teeth? — surely not in the stomach? — nevertheless, such is their situation; and these are not mere appendages, that are called teeth by courtesy, but stout, regular grinding teeth, with a light brown surface. They are not only within the stomach, but fixed to a cartilage nearest to its lower extremity, so that the food, unlike that of other creatures, is submitted to the action of the teeth as it is passing *from* the stomach, instead of being chewed before it is swallowed. In some species the teeth are five in number; but throughout this class of animals the same general principle of construction may be observed. Crabs and their kindred have no brain, because they are not required to reason upon what they observe: they have a nervous system excellently suited to their mode of life, and its knots or ganglia send out nerves to the organs of sense, digestion, motion, etc. The senses of these beings are very acute, especially their sight, hearing, and smell. Most of my readers have heard of crabs' eyes, or have seen these organs in the animal on the end of two little projecting knobs, above and on each side of the mouth: few of them, however, have seen the crab's ear; yet it is very easily found, and is a little triangular bump placed near the base of the feelers. This bump has a membrane stretched over it, and communicates with a small cavity, which is the internal ear. The *organ* of smell is not so easily demonstrated as that of hearing, though the evidence of their possessing the sense to an acute degree is readily attainable. A German naturalist inferred, from the fact of the nerve corresponding to the olfactory nerve in man being distributed to the antennæ, in insects, that the antennæ were the organs of smell in them. Cuvier and others suggest that a similar arrangement may exist in the crustacea. To satisfy myself whether it was so or not, I lately dissected a small lobster, and was delighted to find that the first pair of nerves actually went to the antennæ, and gave positive support to the opinion mentioned. I state this, not to claim credit for ascertaining the truth or inaccuracies of a suggestion, but with a view of inviting the reader to do the same in all cases of doubt. Where it is possible to refer to *nature* for the actual condition of facts, learned *authorities* give me no uneasiness. If I find that the structure bears out their opinions, it is more satisfactory; when it convicts them of absurdity, it saves much fruitless reading, as well as the trouble of shaking off prejudices.

The first time my attention was called to the extreme acuteness of sight possessed by these animals, was during a walk along the flats of Long Island, reaching towards Governor's Island, in New York. A vast number of the small land-crabs, called fiddlers by the boys (*gecarcinus*), occupy burrows or caves dug in the marshy soil, whence they come out and go for some distance, either in search of food or to sun themselves. Long before I approached close enough to see their forms with distinctness, they were scampering towards their holes, into which they plunged with a tolerable certainty of escape — these retreats being of considerable depth, and often communicating with each other, as well as nearly filled with water. On endeavouring cautiously to approach some others, it was quite amusing to observe their vigilance — to see them slowly change position, and, from lying extended in the sun, beginning to gather themselves up for a start, should it prove necessary: at length standing up, as it were, on tiptoe, and raising their pedunculated eyes as high as possible. One quick step on the part of the individual approaching was enough — away they would go, with a celerity which must appear surprising to any one who had not previously witnessed it. What is more remarkable, they possess the power of moving equally well with any part of the body foremost; so that, when endeavouring to escape, they will suddenly dart off to one side or the other, without turning round, and thus elude pursuit. My observations upon the crustaceous animals have extended through many years, and in very various situations; and for the sake of making the general view of their qualities more satisfactory, I will go on to state what I remarked of some of the genera and species in the West Indies, where they are exceedingly numerous and various. The greater proportion of the genera feed on animal matter, especially after decomposition has begun: a large number are exclusively confined to the deep waters, and approach the shoals and lands only during the spawning season. Many live in the sea, but daily pass many hours upon the rocky shores for the pleasure of basking in the sun; others live in marshy or moist ground, at a considerable distance from the water, and feed principally on vegetable food, especially the sugar-cane, of which they are extremely destructive. Others, again, reside habitually on the hills or mountains, and visit the sea only once a year, for the purpose of depositing their eggs in the sand. All those which reside in burrows made in moist ground, and those coming daily on the rocks to bask in the sun, participate in about an equal degree in the qualities of vigilance and swiftness. Many a breathless race have I run in vain, attempting to intercept them, and prevent their escaping into the sea. Many an hour of cautious and solicitous endeavour to steal upon them unobserved, has been frustrated by their long-sighted watchfulness; and several times, when, by extreme care and cunning approaches, I have actually succeeded in getting between a fine specimen and the sea, and had full hope of driving him farther inland, have all my anticipations been ruined by the wonderful swiftness of their flight, or the surprising facility with which they would dart off in the very opposite direction, at the very moment I felt almost sure of my prize. One day, in particular, I saw on a flat rock, which afforded a fine sunning place, the most beautiful crab I had ever beheld. It was of the largest size, and would have covered a large dinner-plate, most beautifully coloured with bright crimson below, and a variety of tints of blue, purple, and green above: it was just such a specimen as could not fail to excite all the solicitude of a collector to obtain. But it was not in the least deficient in the art of self-preservation: my most careful manœuvres proved ineffectual, and all my efforts only enabled me to see enough of it to augment my regrets to a high degree. Subsequently, I saw a similar individual in the collection of a resident: this had been killed against the rocks during a violent hurricane, with very slight injury to its shell. I offered high rewards to the black people if they would bring me such a one, but the most expert among them seemed to think it an unpromising search, as they knew of no way of capturing them. If I had been supplied with some powder of nux vomica, with which to poison some meat, I *might* have succeeded.

JOHN.

No. VIII.

The fleet running crab (*cypoda pugilator*), mentioned as living in burrows dug in a moist soil, and preying chiefly on the sugar-cane, is justly regarded as one of the most noxious pests that can infest a plantation. Their burrows extend to a great depth, and run in various directions; they are also, like those of our fiddlers, nearly full of muddy water, so that, when these marauders once plump into their dens, they may be considered as entirely beyond pursuit. Their numbers are so great, and they multiply in such numbers, as in some seasons to destroy a large proportion of a sugar crop; and sometimes their ravages, combined with those of the rats and other plunderers, are absolutely ruinous to the seaside planters. I was shown, by the superintendant of a place thus infested, a great quantity of cane utterly killed by these creatures, which cut it off in a peculiar manner, in order to suck the juice; and he assured me that, during that season, the crop would be two-thirds less than its average, solely owing to the inroads of the crabs and rats, which, if possible, are still more numerous. It was to me an irresistible source of amusement to observe the air of spite and vexation with which he spoke of the crabs: the rats he could shoot, poison, or drive off for a time with dogs. But the crabs would not eat his poison, while sugar-cane was growing; the dogs could only chase them into their holes; and if, in helpless irritation, he sometimes fired his gun at a cluster of them, the shot only rattled over their shells like hail against a window. It is truly desirable that some summary mode of lessening their number could be devised, and it is probable that this will be best effected by poison, as it may be possible to obtain a bait sufficiently attractive to ensnare them. Species of this genus are found in various parts of our country, more especially towards the south. About Cape May, our friends may have excellent opportunities of testing the truth of what is said of their swiftness and vigilance.

The land-crab, which is common to many of the West India Islands, is more generally known as the Jamaica crab, because it has been most frequently described from observation in that island. Wherever found, they have all the habit of living, during great part of the year, in the highlands, where they pass the day-time concealed in huts, cavities, and under stones, and come out at night for their food. They are remarkable for collecting in vast bodies, and marching annually to the sea-side, in order to deposit their eggs in the sand; and this accomplished, they return to their former abodes, if undisturbed. They commence their march in the night, and move in the most direct line towards the destined point. So obstinately do they pursue this route, that they will not turn out of it for any obstacle that can possibly be surmounted. During the day-time they skulk and lie hid as closely as possible, but thousands upon thousands of them are taken for the use of the table, by whites and blacks, as on their seaward march they are very fat, and of fine flavour. On the homeward journey, those that have escaped capture are weak, exhausted, and unfit for use. Before dismissing the crabs, I must mention one which was a source of much annoyance to me at first, and of considerable interest afterwards, from the observation of its habits. At that time I resided in a house delightfully situated about two hundred yards from the sea, fronting the setting sun, having in clear weather the lofty mountains of Porto Rico, distant about eighty miles, in view. Like most of the houses in the island, ours had seen better days, as was evident from various breaks in the floors, angles rotted off the doors, sunken sills, and other indications of decay. Our sleeping room, which was on the lower floor, was especially in this condition; but as the weather was delightfully warm, a few cracks and openings, though rather large, did not threaten much inconvenience. Our bed was provided with that indispensable accompaniment, a musquito bar or curtain, to which we were indebted for escape from various annoyances. Scarcely had we extinguished the light, and composed ourselves to rest, when we heard, in various parts of the room, the most startling noises. It appeared as if numerous hard and heavy bodies were trailed along the floor; then they sounded as if climbing up by the chairs and other furniture, and frequently something like a large stone would tumble down from such elevations, with a loud noise, followed by a peculiar chirping noise. What an effect this produced upon entirely inexperienced strangers, may well be imagined by those who have been suddenly waked up in the dark, by some unaccountable noise in the room. Finally, these invaders began to ascend the bed; but happily the musquito bar was securely tucked under the bed all around, and they were denied access, though their efforts and tumbles to the floor produced no very comfortable reflections. Towards day-light they began to retire, and in the morning no trace of any such visitants could be perceived. On mentioning our troubles, we were told that this nocturnal disturber was only Bernard the Hermit, called generally the soldier-crab, perhaps from the peculiar habit he has of protecting his body by thrusting it into any empty shell, which he afterwards carries about until he outgrows it, when it is relinquished for a larger. Not choosing to pass another night quite so noisily, due care was taken to exclude Monsieur Bernard, whose knockings were thenceforward confined to the outside of the house. I baited a large wire rat-trap with some corn-meal, and placed it outside of the back door, and in the morning found it literally half filled with these crabs, from the largest-sized shell that could enter the trap, down to such as were not larger than a hickory-nut. Here was a fine collection made at once, affording a very considerable variety in the size and age of the specimens, and the different shells into which they had introduced themselves.

The soldier or hermit-crab, when withdrawn from his adopted shell, presents, about the head and claws, a considerable family resemblance to the lobster. The claws, however, are very short and broad, and the body covered with hard shell only in that part which is liable to be exposed or protruded. The posterior or abdominal part of the body is covered only by a tough skin, and tapers towards a small extremity, furnished with a sort of hook-like apparatus, enabling it to hold on to its factitious dwelling. Along the surface of its abdomen, as well as on the back, there are small projections, apparently intended for the same purpose. When once fairly in possession of a shell, it would be quite a difficult matter to pull the crab out, though a very little heat applied to the shell will quickly induce him to leave it. The shells they select are taken solely with reference to their suitableness, and hence you may catch a considerable number of the same species, each of which is in a different species or genus of shell. The shells commonly used by them, when of larger size, are those of the whilk, which are much used as an article of food by the islanders, or the smaller conch [strombus] shells. The very young hermit-crabs are found in almost every variety of small shell found on the shores of the Antilles. I have frequently been amused by ladies eagerly engaged in making collections of these beautiful little shells, and not dreaming of their being tenanted by a living animal, suddenly startled, on displaying their acquisitions, by observing them to be actively endeavouring to escape; or, on introducing the hand into the reticule to produce a particularly fine specimen, to receive a smart pinch from the claws of the little hermit. The instant the shell is closely approached or touched, they withdraw as deeply into the shell as possible, and the small ones readily escape observation, but they soon become impatient of captivity, and try to make off. The species of this genus (*pagurus*) are very numerous, and during the first part of their lives are all aquatic; that is, they are hatched in the little pools about the margin of the sea, and remain there until those that are destined to live on land are stout enough to commence their travels. The hermit-crabs, which are altogether aquatic, are by no means so careful to choose the lightest and thinnest shells, as the land troops. The aquatic soldiers may be seen towing along shells of the most disproportionate size; but their relatives, who travel over the hills by moonlight, know that all unnecessary incumbrance of weight should be avoided. They are as pugnacious and spiteful as any of the crustaceous class; and when taken, or when they fall and jar themselves considerably, utter a chirping noise, which is evidently an angry expression. They are ever ready to bite with their claws, and the pinch of the larger individuals is quite painful. It is said that, when they are changing their shells, for the sake of obtaining more commodious coverings, they frequently fight for possession, which may be true where two that have forsaken their old shells meet, or happen to make choice of the same vacant one. It is also said, that one crab is sometimes forced to give up the shell he is in, should a stronger chance to desire it. This, as I never saw it, I must continue to doubt; for I cannot imagine how the stronger could possibly accomplish his purpose, seeing that the occupant has nothing to do but keep close quarters. The invader would have no chance of seizing him to pull him out, nor could he do him any injury by biting upon the surface of his hard claws, the only part that would be exposed. If it be true that one can dispossess the other, it must be by some contrivance of which we are still ignorant. These soldier-crabs feed on a great variety of substances, scarcely refusing anything that is edible: like the family they belong to, they have a decided partiality for putrid meats, and the planters accuse them also of too great a fondness for the sugar-cane. Their excursions are altogether nocturnal: in the day-time they lie concealed very effectually in small holes, among stones, or any kind of rubbish, and are rarely taken notice of, even where hundreds are within a short distance of each other. The larger soldier-crabs are sometimes eaten by the blacks, but they are not much sought after even by them, as they are generally regarded with aversion and prejudice. There is no reason, that we are aware of, why they should not be as good as many other crabs, but they certainly are not equally esteemed.

JOHN.

No. IX.

Those who have only lived in forest countries, where vast tracts are shaded by a dense growth of oak, ash, chestnut, hickory, and other trees of deciduous foliage, which present the most pleasing varieties of verdure and freshness, can have but little idea of the effect produced on the feelings by aged forests of pine, composed in a great degree of a single species, whose towering summits are crowned with one dark green canopy, which successive seasons find unchanged, and nothing but death causes to vary. Their robust and gigantic trunks rise an hundred or more feet high, in purely proportioned columns, before the limbs begin to diverge; and their tops, densely clothed with long, bristling foliage, intermingle so closely as to allow of but slight entrance to the sun. Hence, the undergrowth of such forests is comparatively slight and thin, since none but shrubs, and plants that love the shade, can flourish under this perpetual exclusion of the animating and invigorating rays of the great exciter of the vegetable world. Through such forests, and by the merest foot-paths, in great part, it was my lot to pass many miles almost every day; and had I not endeavoured to derive some amusement and instruction from the study of the forest itself, my time would have been as fatiguing to me, as it was certainly quiet and solemn. But wherever nature is, and under whatever form she may present herself, enough is always proffered to fix attention and produce pleasure, if we will condescend to observe with carefulness. I soon found that even a pine-forest was far from being devoid of interest, and shall endeavour to prove this by stating the result of various observations made during the time I lived in this situation.

The common pitch, or, as it is generally called, Norway pine, grows from a seed, which is matured in vast abundance in the large cones peculiar to the pines. This seed is of a rather triangular shape, thick and heavy at the part by which it grows from the cone, and terminating in a broad membranous fan or sail, which, when the seeds are shaken out by the wind, enables them to sail obliquely through the air to great distances. Should an old corn-field, or other piece of ground, be thrown out of cultivation for more than one season, it is sown with pine-seeds by the winds, and the young pines shoot up as closely and compactly as hemp. They continue to grow in this manner until they become twelve or fifteen feet high, until their roots begin to encroach on each other, or until the stoutest and best rooted begin to overtop so as entirely to shade the smaller. These gradually begin to fail, and finally dry up and perish, and a similar process is continued until the best trees acquire room enough to grow without impediment. Even when the young pines have attained to thirty or forty feet in height, and are as thick as a man's thigh, they stand so closely together that their lower branches, which are all dry and dead, are intermingled sufficiently to prevent any one from passing between the trees, without first breaking these obstructions away. I have seen such a wood as that just mentioned, covering an old corn-field, whose ridges were still distinctly to be traced, and which an old resident informed me he had seen growing in corn. In a part of this wood, which was not far from my dwelling, I had a delightful retreat, that served me as a private study or closet, though enjoying all the advantages of the open air. A road that had once passed through the field, and was of course more compacted than any other part, had denied access to the pine-seeds for a certain distance, while on each side of it they grew with their usual density. The ground was covered with the soft layer or carpet of dried pine leaves which gradually and imperceptibly fall throughout the year, making a most pleasant surface to tread on, and rendering the step perfectly noiseless. By beating off with a stick all the dried branches that projected towards the vacant space, I formed a sort of chamber, fifteen or twenty feet long, which above was canopied by the densely-mingled branches of the adjacent trees, which altogether excluded or scattered the rays of the sun, and on all sides was so shut in by the trunks of the young trees, as to prevent all observation. Hither, during the hot season, I was accustomed to retire for the purpose of reading or meditation; and within this deeper solitude, where all was solitary, very many of the subsequent movements of my life were suggested or devised.

From all I could observe, and all the inquiries I could get answered, it appeared that this rapidly-growing tree does not attain its full growth until it is eighty or ninety years old, nor does its time of full health and vigour much exceed an hundred. Before this time it is liable to the attacks of insects, but these are of a kind that bore the tender spring shoots to deposit their eggs therein, and their larvæ appear to live principally on the sap, which is very abundant, so that the tree is but slightly injured. But after the pine has attained its acmé, it is attacked by an insect which deposits its egg in the body of the tree, and the larva devours its way through the solid substance of the timber; so that, after a pine has been for one or two seasons subjected to these depredators, it will be fairly riddled, and, if cut down, is unfit for any other purpose than burning. Indeed, if delayed too long, it is poorly fit for fire-wood, so thoroughly do these insects destroy its substance. At the same time that one set of insects is engaged in destroying the body, myriads of others are at work under the bark, destroying the sap vessels, and the foliage wears a more and more pale and sickly appearance as the tree declines in vigour. If not cut down, it eventually dies, becomes leafless, stripped of its bark, and, as the decay advances, all the smaller branches are broken off; and it stands with its naked trunk and a few ragged limbs, as if bidding defiance to the tempest which howls around its head. Under favourable circumstances, a large trunk will stand in this condition for nearly a century, so extensive and powerful are its roots, so firm and stubborn the original knitting of its giant frame. At length some storm, more furious than all its predecessors, wrenches those ponderous roots from the soil, and hurls the helpless carcass to the earth, crushing all before it in its fall. Without the aid of fire, or some peculiarity of situation favourable to rapid decomposition, full another hundred years will be requisite to reduce it to its elements, and obliterate the traces of its existence. Indeed, long after the lapse of more than that period, we find the heart of the pitch-pine still preserving its original form, and, from being thoroughly imbued with turpentine, become utterly indestructible except by fire.

If the proprietor attend to the warnings afforded by the wood-pecker, he may always cut his pines in time to prevent them from being injured by insects. The wood-peckers run up and around the trunks, tapping from time to time with their powerful bill. The bird knows at once by the sound whether there be insects below or not. If the tree is sound, the wood-pecker soon forsakes it for another: should he begin to break into the bark, it is to catch the worm; and such trees are at once to be marked for the axe In felling such pines, I found the woodmen always anxious to avoid letting them strike against neighbouring sound trees, as they said that the insects more readily attacked an injured tree than one whose bark was unbroken. The observation is most probably correct; at least the experience of country folks in such matters is rarely wrong, though they sometimes give very odd reasons for the processes they adopt.

A full-grown pine-forest is at all times a grand and majestic object to one accustomed to moving through it. Those vast and towering columns, sustaining a waving crown of deepest verdure; those robust and rugged limbs standing forth at a vast height overhead, loaded with the cones of various seasons; and the diminutiveness of all surrounding objects compared with these gigantic children of nature, cannot but inspire ideas of seriousness, and even of melancholy. But how awful and even tremendous does such a situation become, when we hear the first wailings of the gathering storm, as it stoops upon the lofty summits of the pine, and soon increases to a deep hoarse roaring, as the boughs begin to wave in the blast, and the whole tree is forced to sway before its power. In a short time the fury of the wind is at its height, the loftiest trees bend suddenly before it, and scarce regain their upright position ere they are again obliged to cower beneath its violence. Then the tempest literally howls, and amid the tremendous reverberations of thunder, and the blazing glare of the lightning, the unfortunate wanderer hears around him the crash of numerous trees hurled down by the storm, and knows not but the next may be precipitated upon him. More than once have I witnessed all the grandeur, dread, and desolation of such a scene, and have always found safety either by seeking as quickly as possible a spot where there were none but young

9*

trees, or, if on a main road, choosing the most open and exposed situation out of the reach of the large trees. There, seated on my horse, who seemed to understand the propriety of such patience, I would quietly remain, however thoroughly drenched, until the fury of the wind was completely over. To say nothing of the danger from falling trees, the peril of being struck by the lightning, which so frequently shivers the loftiest of them, is so great as to render any attempt to advance at such time highly imprudent.

Like the ox among animals, the pine-tree may be looked upon as one of the most universally useful of the sons of the forest. For all sorts of building, for firewood, tar, turpentine, rosin, lamp-black, and a vast variety of other useful products, this tree is invaluable to man. Nor is it a pleasing contemplation, to one who knows its usefulness, to observe to how vast an amount it is annually destroyed in this country, beyond the proportion that nature can possibly supply. However, we are not disposed to believe that this evil will ever be productive of very great injury, especially as coal fuel is becoming annually more extensively used. Nevertheless, were I the owner of a pine-forest, I should exercise a considerable degree of care in the selection of the wood for the axe.

JOHN.

No. X.

Among the enemies with which the farmers of a poor or light soil have to contend, I know of none so truly formidable and injurious as the crows, whose numbers, cunning, and audacity can scarcely be appreciated, except by those who have had long-continued and numerous opportunities of observation. Possessed of the most acute senses, and endowed by nature with a considerable share of reasoning power, these birds bid defiance to almost all the contrivances resorted to for their destruction; and when their numbers have accumulated to vast multitudes, which annually occurs, it is scarcely possible to estimate the destruction they are capable of effecting. Placed in a situation where every object was subjected to close observation, as a source of amusement, it is not surprising that my attention should be drawn to so conspicuous an object as the crow; and having once commenced remarking the peculiarities of this bird, I continued to bestow attention upon it during many years, in whatever situation it was met with. The thickly-wooded and well-watered parts of the State of Maryland, as affording them a great abundance of food, and almost entire security during their breeding season, are especially infested by these troublesome creatures, so that at some times of the year they are collected in numbers which would appear incredible to any one unaccustomed to witness their accumulations.

Individually, the common crow (*corvus corona*) may be compared in character with the brown or Norway rat, being, like that quadruped, addicted to all sorts of mischief, destroying the lives of any small creatures that may fall in its way, plundering with audacity wherever anything is exposed to its rapaciousness, and triumphing by its cunning over the usual artifices employed for the destruction of ordinary noxious animals. Where food is at any time scarce, or the opportunity for such marauding inviting, there is scarcely a young animal about the farm-yards safe from the attacks of the crow. Young chickens, ducks, goslings, and even little pigs, when quite young and feeble, are carried off by them. They are not less eager to discover the nests of domestic fowls; and will sit very quietly in sight, at a convenient distance, until the hen leaves the nest, and then fly down and suck her eggs at leisure. But none of their tricks excited in me a greater interest, than the observation of their attempts to rob a hen of her chicks. The crow, alighting at a little distance from the hen, would advance in an apparently careless way towards the brood, when the vigilant parent would bristle up her feathers, and rush at the black rogue to drive him off. After several such approaches, the hen would become very angry, and would chase the crow to a greater distance from the brood. This is the very object the robber has in view, for, as long as the parent keeps near her young, the crow has very slight chance of success; but as soon as he can induce her to follow him to a little distance from the brood, he takes advantage of his wings, and, before she can regain her place, has flown over her, and seized one of her chickens. When the cock is present, there is still less danger from such an attack, for chanticleer shows all his vigilance and gallantry in protecting his tender offspring, though it frequently happens that the number of hens with broods renders it impossible for him to extend his care to all. When the crow tries to carry off a gosling from the mother, it requires more daring and skill, and is far less frequently successful than in the former instance. If the gander be in company, which he almost uniformly is, the crow has his labour in vain. Notwithstanding the advantages of flight and superior cunning, the honest vigilance and determined bravery of the former are too much for him. His attempts to approach, however cautiously conducted, are promptly met, and all his tricks rendered unavailing, by the fierce movements of the gander, whose powerful blows the crow seems to be well aware might effectually disable him. The first time I witnessed such a scene, I was at the side of the creek, and saw on the opposite shore a goose with her goslings, beset by a crow: from the apparent alarm of the mother and brood, it seemed to me they must be in great danger, and I called to the owner of the place, who happened to be in sight, to inform him of their situation. Instead of going to their relief, he shouted back to me, to ask if the gander was not there too; and as soon as he was answered in the affirmative, he bid me be under no uneasiness, as the crow would find his match. Nothing could exceed the cool impudence and pertinacity of the crow, who, perfectly regardless of my shouting, continued to worry the poor gander for an hour, by his efforts to obtain a nice gosling for his next meal. At length, convinced of the fruitlessness of his efforts, he flew off to seek some more easily procurable food. Several crows sometimes unite to plunder the goose of her young, and are then generally successful, because they are able to distract the attention of the parents, and lure them farther from their young.

In the summer the crows disperse in pairs, for the purpose of raising their young, and then they select lofty trees in the remotest parts of the forest, upon which, with dry sticks and twigs, they build a large strong nest, and line it with softer materials. They lay four or five eggs, and, when they are hatched, feed, attend, and watch over their young with the most zealous devotion. Should any one by chance pass near the nest while the eggs are still unhatched, or the brood are very young, the parents keep close, and neither by the slightest movement nor noise betray their presence. But if the young are fledged, and beginning to take their first lessons in flying, the approach of a man, especially if armed with a gun, calls forth all their cunning and solicitude. The young are immediately placed in the securest place at hand, where the foliage is thickest, and remain perfectly motionless and quiet. Not so the alarmed parents, both of which fly nearer and nearer to the hunter, uttering the most discordant screams, with an occasional peculiar note, which seems intended to direct or warn their young. So close do they approach, and so clamorous are they as the hunter endeavours to get a good view of them on the tree, that he is almost uniformly persuaded the young crows are also concealed there; but he does not perceive, as he is cautiously trying to get within gun-shot, that they are moving from tree to tree, and at each remove are farther and farther from the place where the young are hid. After continuing this trick until it is impossible that the hunter can retain any idea of the situation of the young ones, the parents cease their distressing outcries, fly quietly to the most convenient lofty tree, and calmly watch the movements of their disturber. Now and then they utter a loud quick cry, which seems intended to bid their offspring lie close and keep quiet, and it is very generally the case that they escape all danger by their obedience. An experienced crow-killer watches eagerly for the tree where the crows first start from; and if this can be observed, he pays no attention to their clamours, nor pretence of throwing themselves in his way, as he is satisfied they are too vigilant to let him get a shot at them; and if he can see the young, he is tolerably sure of them all, because of their inability to fly or change place readily.

The time of the year in which the farmers suffer

most from them, is in the spring, before their enormous congregations disperse, and when they are rendered voracious by the scantiness of their winter fare. Woe betide the corn-field which is not closely watched, when the young grain begins to shoot above the soil! If not well guarded, a host of these marauders will settle upon it at the first light of the dawn, and before the sun has risen far above the horizon, will have plundered every shoot of the germinating seed, by first drawing it skilfully from the moist earth by the young stalk, and then swallowing the grain. The negligent or careless planter, who does not visit his fields before breakfast, finds, on his arrival, that he must either replant his corn, or relinquish hopes of a crop; and, without the exertion of due vigilance, he may be obliged to repeat this process twice or thrice the same season. Where the crows go to rob a field in this way, they place one or more sentinels, according to circumstances, in convenient places; and these are exceedingly vigilant, uttering a single warning call, which puts the whole to flight the instant there is the least appearance of danger or interruption. Having fixed their sentinels, they begin regularly at one part of the field, and pursuing the rows along, pulling up each shoot in succession, and biting off the corn at the root. The green shoots thus left along the rows, as if they had been arranged with care, offer a melancholy memorial of the work which has been effected by these cunning and destructive plunderers.

Numerous experiments have been made, where

the crows are thus injurious, to avert their ravages; and the method I shall now relate I have seen tried with the most gratifying success. In a large tub a portion of tar and grease were mixed, so as to render the tar sufficiently thin and soft, and to this was added a portion of slacked lime in powder, and the whole stirred until thoroughly incorporated. The seed-corn was then thrown in, and stirred with the mixture until each grain received a uniform coating. The corn was then dropped in the hills, and covered as usual. This treatment was found to retard the germination about three days, as the mixture greatly excludes moisture from the grain. But the crows did no injury to the field: they pulled up a small quantity in different parts of the planting, to satisfy themselves it was all alike; upon becoming convinced of which, they quietly left it for some less carefully managed grounds, where pains had not been taken to make all the corn so nauseous and bitter.

JOHN.

No. XI.

It rarely happens that any of the works of nature are wholly productive of evil; and even the crows, troublesome as they are, contribute in a small degree to the good of the district they frequent. Thus, though they destroy eggs and young poultry, plunder the corn-fields, and carry off whatever may serve for food, they also rid the surface of the earth of a considerable quantity of carrion, and a vast multitude of insects and their destructive larvæ. The crows are very usefully employed when they alight upon newly-ploughed fields, and pick up great numbers of those large and long-lived worms which are so destructive to the roots of all growing vegetables; and they are scarcely less so when they follow the seine-haulers along the shores, and pick up the small fishes, which would otherwise be left to putrefy, and load the air with unpleasant vapours. Nevertheless, they become far more numerous in some parts of the country than is at all necessary to the good of the inhabitants, and whoever would devise a method of lessening their numbers suddenly, would certainly be doing a service to the community.

About a quarter of a mile above the house I lived in, on Curtis's creek, the shore was a sandbank or bluff, twenty or thirty feet high, crowned with a dense young pine-forest to its very edge. Almôst directly opposite, the shore was flat, and formed a point, extending, in the form of a broad sand-bar, for a considerable distance into the water; and, when the tide was low, this flat afforded a fine level space, to which nothing could approach in either direction without being easily seen. At a short distance from the water, a young swamp-wood of maple, gum, oaks, etc. extended back towards some higher ground. As the sun descended, and threw his last rays in one broad sheet of golden effulgence over the crystal mirror of the waters, innumerable companies of crows arrived daily, and settled on this point, for the purpose of drinking, picking up gravel, and uniting in one body prior to retiring for the night to their accustomed dormitory. The trees adjacent and all the shore would be literally blackened by these plumed marauders, while their increasing outcries, chattering, and screams, were almost deafening. It certainly seems that they derive great pleasure from their social habits; and I often amused myself by thinking the uninterrupted clatter which was kept up, as the different gangs united with the main body, was produced by the recital of the adventures they had encountered during their last marauding excursions. As the sun became entirely sunk below the horizon, the grand flock crossed to the sand-bluff on the opposite side, where they generally spent a few moments in picking up a farther supply of gravel, and then, arising in dense and ample column, they sought their habitual roost in the deep entanglements of the distant pines. This daily visit to the point, so near to my dwelling, and so accessible by means of the skiff, led me to hope that I should have considerable success in destroying them. Full of such anticipations, I loaded two guns, and proceeded in my boat to the expected place of action, previous to the arrival of the crows. My view was to have my boat somewhere about half-way between the two shores, and (as they never manifested much fear of boats) to take my chance of firing upon the main body as they were flying over my head to the opposite side of the river. Shortly after I had gained my station, the companies began to arrive, and everything went on as usual. But whether they suspected some mischief from seeing a boat so long stationary in their vicinity, or could see and distinguish the guns in the boat, I am unable to say: the fact was, however, that when they set out to fly over, they passed at an elevation which secured them from my artillery effectually, although, on ordinary occasions, they were in the habit of flying over me at a height of not more than twenty or thirty feet. I returned home without having had a shot, but resolved to try if I could not succeed better the next day. The same result followed the experiment, and when I fired at one gang, which it appeared possible to attain, the instant the gun was discharged the crows made a sort of halt, descended considerably, flying in circles, and screaming most vociferously, as if in contempt or derision. Had I been prepared for this, a few of them might have suffered for their bravado. But my second gun was in the bow of the boat, and before I could get to it the black gentry had risen to their former security. While we were sitting at tea that evening, a black came to inform me that a considerable flock of crows, which had arrived too late to join the great flock, had pitched in the young pines, not a great way from the house, and at a short distance from the road-side. We quickly had the guns in readiness, and I scarcely could restrain my impatience until it should be late enough and dark enough to give us a chance of success. Without thinking of anything but the great number of the crows, and their inability to fly to advantage in the night, my notions of the numbers we should bring home were extravagant enough, and I only regretted that we might be obliged to leave some behind. At length, led by the black boy, we sallied forth, and soon arrived in the vicinity of this temporary and unusual roost; and now the true character of the enterprise began to appear. We were to leave the road, and penetrate several hundred yards among the pines, whose proximity to each other, and the difficulty of moving between which, on account of the dead branches, has been heretofore stated. Next, we had to be careful not to alarm the crows before we were ready to act, and at the same time were to advance with cocked guns in our hands. The only way of moving forwards at all, I found to be that of turning my shoulders as much as possible to the dead branches, and breaking my way as gently as I could. At last we reached the trees upon which the crows were roosting; but as the foliage of the young pines was extremely dense, and the birds were full forty feet above the ground, it was out of the question to distinguish where the greatest number were situated. Selecting the trees which appeared by the greater darkness of their summits to be most heavily laden with our game, my companion and I pulled our triggers at the same moment. The report was followed by considerable outcries from the crows, by a heavy shower of pine twigs and leaves upon which the shot had taken effect, and a deafening roar, caused by the sudden rising on the wing of the alarmed sleepers. *One* crow at length fell near me, which was wounded too badly to fly or retain his perch, and as the flock had gone entirely off, with this one crow did I return, rather crest-fallen, from my grand nocturnal expedition. This crow, however, afforded me instructive employment and amusement, during the next day, in the dissection of its nerves and organs of sense; and I know not that I ever derived more pleasure from any anatomical examination, than I did from the dissection of its internal ear. The extent and convolutions of its semi-circular canals show how highly the sense of hearing is perfected in these creatures; and those who wish to be convinced of the truth of what we have stated in relation to them, may still see this identical crow skull in the Baltimore Museum, to which I presented it after finishing the dissection. At least, I saw it there a year or two since; though I little thought, when employed in examining, or even when I last saw it, that it would ever be the subject of such a reference, "in a printed book."

Not easily disheartened by preceding failures, I next resolved to try to outwit the crows, and for this purpose prepared a long line, to which a very considerable number of lateral lines were tied, having each a very small fish-hook at the end. Each of these hooks was baited with a single grain of corn, so cunningly put on, that it seemed impossible that the grain could be taken up without the hook being swallowed with it. About four o'clock, in order to be in full time, I rowed up to the sandy point, made fast my main line to a bush, and extending it toward the water, pegged it down at the other end securely in the sand. I next arranged all my baited lines, and then, covering them all nicely with sand, left nothing exposed but the bait. This done, I scattered a quantity of corn all around, to render the baits as little liable to suspicion as possible. After taking a final view of the arrangement, which seemed a very hopeful one, I pulled my boat gently homeward, to wait the event of my solicitude for the capture of the crows. As usual, they arrived in thousands, blackened the sand beach, chattered, screamed, and fluttered about in great glee, and finally sailed over the creek and away to their roost, without having left a solitary unfortunate to pay for having meddled with my baited hooks. I jumped into the skiff, and soon paid a visit to my unsuccessful snare. The corn was all gone; the very hooks were all bare; and it was evident that some other expedient must be adopted before I could hope to succeed. Had I caught but one or two *alive,* it was my intention to have employed them to procure the destruction of others, in a manner I shall hereafter describe.

JOHN.

No. XII.

Had I succeeded in obtaining some living crows, they were to be employed in the following manner: After having made a sort of concealment of brushwood within good gun-shot distance, the crows were to be fastened by their wings on their backs between two pegs, yet not so closely as to prevent them from fluttering or struggling. The other crows, who are always very inquisitive where their species is in any trouble, were expected to light down near the captives, and the latter would certainly seize the first that came near enough with their claws, and hold on pertinaciously. This would have produced fighting and screaming in abundance, and the whole flock might gradually be so drawn into the fray, as to allow many opportunities of discharging the guns upon them with full effect. This I have often observed—that when a quarrel or fight took place in a large flock or gang of crows (a circumstance by no means infrequent), it seemed soon to extend to the whole; and during the continuance of their anger all the usual caution of their nature appeared to be forgotten, allowing themselves at such times to be approached closely; and, regardless of men, firearms, or the fall of their companions, continuing their wrangling with rancorous obstinacy. A similar disposition may be produced among them by catching a large owl, and tying it with a cord of moderate length to the limb of a naked tree in a neighbourhood frequented by the crows. The owl is one of the few enemies which the crow has much reason to dread, as it robs the nests of their young, whenever they are left for the shortest time. Hence, whenever crows discover an owl in the day-time, like many other birds, they commence an attack upon it, screaming most vociferously, and bringing together all of their species within hearing. Once this clamour has fairly begun, and their passions are fully aroused, there is little danger of their being scared away, and the chance of destroying them by shooting is continued as long as the owl remains uninjured. But one such opportunity presented during my residence where crows were abundant, and this was unfortunately spoiled by the eagerness of one of the gunners, who, in his eagerness to demolish one of the crows, fixed upon some that were most busy with the owl, and killed it instead of its disturbers, which at once ended the sport. When the crows leave the roost, at early dawn, they generally fly to a naked or leafless tree in the nearest field, and there plume themselves and chatter until the day-light is sufficiently clear to show all objects with distinctness. Of this circumstance I have taken advantage several times, to get good shots at them in this way. During the day-time, having selected a spot within proper distance of the tree frequented by them in the morning, I have built with brushwood and pine-bushes a thick, close screen, behind which one or two persons might move securely without being observed. Proper openings through which to level the guns were also made, as the slightest stir or noise could not be made, at the time of action, without a risk of rendering all the preparations fruitless. The guns were all in order and loaded before going to bed, and at an hour or two before day-light we repaired quietly to the field, and stationed ourselves behind the screen, where, having mounted our guns at the loop-holes, to be in perfect readiness, we waited patiently for the day-break. Soon after the gray twilight of the dawn began to displace the darkness, the voice of one of our expected visitants would be heard from the distant forest, and shortly after a single crow would slowly sail towards the solitary tree, and settle on its very summit. Presently a few more would arrive singly, and in a little while small flocks followed. Conversation among them is at first rather limited to occasional salutations, but as the flock begins to grow numerous, it becomes general and very animated, and by this time all that may be expected on this occasion have arrived. This may be known, also, by observing one or more of them descend to the ground, and if the gunners do not now make the best of the occasion, it will soon be lost, as the whole gang will presently sail off, scattering as they go. However, we rarely waited till there was a danger of their departure, but as soon as the flock had fairly arrived, and were still crowded upon the upper parts of the tree, we pulled triggers together, aiming at the thickest of the throng. In this way, by killing and wounding them, with two or three guns, a dozen or more would be destroyed. It was of course needless to expect to find a similar opportunity in the same place for a long time afterwards, as those which escaped had too good memories to return to so disastrous a spot. By ascertaining other situations at considerable distances, we could every now and then obtain similar advantages over them.

About the years 1800–1–2–3–4, the crows were so vastly accumulated and destructive in the State of Maryland, that the government, to hasten their diminution, received their heads in payment of taxes, at the price of three cents each. The storekeepers bought them of the boys and shooters, who had no taxes to pay, at a rather lower rate, or exchanged powder and shot for them. This measure caused a great havoc to be kept up among them, and in a few years so much diminished the grievance, that the price was withdrawn. Two modes of shooting them in considerable numbers were followed, and with great success: the one, that of killing them while on the wing towards the roost; and the other, attacking them in the night, when they have been for some hours asleep. I have already mentioned the regularity with which vast flocks move from various quarters of the country to their roosting-places every afternoon, and the uniformity of the route they pursue. In cold weather, when all the small bodies of water are frozen, and they are obliged to protract their flight towards the bays or sea, their return is a work of considerable labour, especially should a strong wind blow against them: at this season, also, being rather poorly fed, they are of necessity less vigorous. Should the wind be adverse, they fly as near the earth as possible, and of this the shooters, at the time I allude to, took advantage. A large number would collect on such an afternoon, and station themselves close along the foot-way of a high bank, over which the crows were in the habit of flying; and as they were in a great degree screened from sight as the flock flew over, keeping as low as possible, because of the wind, their shots were generally very effectual. The stronger was the wind, the greater was their success. The crows that were not injured found it very difficult to rise, and those that diverged laterally only came nearer to gunners stationed in expectation of such movements. The flocks were several hours in passing over; and as there was generally a considerable interval between each company of considerable size, the last arrived, unsuspicious of what had been going on, and the shooters had time to recharge their arms. But the grand harvest of crow heads was derived from the invasion of their dormitories, which are well worthy a particular description, and should be visited by every one who wishes to form a proper idea of the number of these birds that may be accumulated in a single district. The roost is most commonly the densest pine-thicket that can be found, generally at no great distance from some river, bay, or other sheet of water, which is the last to freeze, or rarely is altogether frozen. To such a roost the crows, which are, during the day-time, scattered over perhaps more than a hundred miles of circumference, wing their way every afternoon, and arrive shortly after sunset. Endless columns pour in from various quarters, and as they arrive pitch upon their accustomed perches, crowding closely together for the benefit of the warmth and the shelter afforded by the thick foliage of the pine. The trees are literally bent by their weight, and the ground is covered for many feet in depth by their dung, which, by its gradual fermentation, must also tend to increase the warmth of the roost. Such roosts are known to be thus occupied for years, beyond the memory of individuals; and I know of one or two which the oldest residents in the quarter state to have been known to their grandfathers, and probably had been resorted to by the crows during several ages previous. There is one of great age and magnificent extent in the vicinity of Rock Creek, an arm of the Patapsco. They are sufficiently numerous on the rivers opening into the Chesapeake, and are everywhere similar in their general aspect. Wilson has signalised such a roost at no great distance from Bristol, Pa.; and I know by observation that not less than a million of crows sleep there nightly during the winter season.

To gather crow heads from the roost, a very large party was made up, proportioned to the extent of surface occupied by the dormitory. Armed with double-barrelled and duck guns, which threw a large charge of shot, the company was divided into small parties, and these took stations, selected during the day-time, so as to surround the roost as nearly as possible. A dark night was always preferred, as the crows could not, when alarmed, fly far, and the attack was delayed until full midnight. All being at their posts, the firing was commenced by those who were most advantageously posted, and followed up successively by the others, as the affrighted crows sought refuge in their vicinity. On every side the carnage then raged fiercely, and there can scarcely be conceived a more forcible idea of the horrors of a battle, than such a scene afforded. The crows screaming with fright and the pain of wounds; the loud deep roar produced by the raising of their whole number in the air; the incessant flashing and thundering of the guns; and the shouts of their eager destroyers, all produced an effect which can never be forgotten by any one who has witnessed it, nor can it well be adequately comprehended by those who have not. Blinded by the blaze of the powder, and bewildered by the thicker darkness that ensues, the crows rise and settle again at a short distance, without being able to withdraw from the field of danger, and the sanguinary work is continued until the shooters are fatigued, or the approach of daylight gives the survivors a chance of escape. Then the work of collecting the heads from the dead and wounded began, and this was a task of considerable difficulty, as the wounded used their utmost efforts to conceal and defend themselves. The bill and half the front of the skull were cut off together, and strung in sums for the tax-gatherer, and the product of the night divided according to the nature of the party formed. Sometimes the great mass of shooters were hired for the night, and received no share of scalps, having their ammunition provided by the employers: other parties were formed of friends and neighbours, who clubbed for the ammunition, and shared equally in the result.

During hard winters the crows suffer greatly, and perish in considerable numbers from hunger. When starved severely, the poor wretches will swallow bits of leather, rope, rags, in short, anything that appears to promise the slightest relief. Multitudes belonging to the Bristol roost perished during the winter of 1828–9 from this cause. All the water-courses were solidly frozen, and it was distressing to observe these starvelings every morning winging their weary way towards the shores of the sea, in hopes of food, and again toiling homewards in the afternoon, apparently scarce able to fly.

In speaking of destroying crows, we have never adverted to the use of poison, which in their case is wholly inadmissible, on this account — where crows are common, hogs generally run at large, and to poison the crows would equally poison them: the crows would die, and fall to the ground, where they would certainly be eaten by the hogs.

Crows, when caught young, learn to talk plainly, if pains be taken to repeat certain phrases to them, and they become exceedingly impudent and troublesome. Like all of their tribe, they will steal and hide silver or other bright objects, of which they can make no possible use. JOHN.

www.ingramcontent.com/pod-product-compliance
Lightning Source LLC
LaVergne TN
LVHW021423110826
845150LV00007B/2061

* 9 7 8 1 4 2 5 5 0 8 9 6 8 *